LIVING PICTURES

THE SUNY SERIES

CULTURAL STUDIES IN CINEMA/VIDEO

Wheeler Winston Dixon, editor

LIVING PICTURES

◼

The Origins
of the Movies

DEAC
ROSSELL

STATE UNIVERSITY OF NEW YORK PRESS

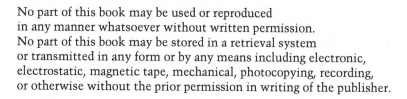

Published by
State University of New York Press, Albany

© 1998 State University of New York

All rights reserved

Printed in the United States of America

No part of this book may be used or reproduced
in any manner whatsoever without written permission.
No part of this book may be stored in a retrieval system
or transmitted in any form or by any means including electronic,
electrostatic, magnetic tape, mechanical, photocopying, recording,
or otherwise without the prior permission in writing of the publisher.

For information, address State University of New York Press,
State University Plaza, Albany, N.Y., 12246

Production by Marilyn P. Semerad
Marketing by Anne M. Valentine

Library of Congress Cataloging-in-Publication Data

Rossell, Deac, 1944–
    Living pictures : the origins of the movies / Deac Rossell.
       p.   cm. — (The SUNY series, cultural studies in cinema/video)
    Includes bibliographical references and index.
    ISBN 0-7914-3767-1 (hc : alk. paper). — ISBN 0-7914-3768-X (pb :
alk. paper)
    1. Cinematography—History. I. Title. II. Series.
    TR848.R68 1998
    778.5'3'09—dc21
                                             94-27561
                                                CIP

10 9 8 7 6 5 4 3 2 1

CONTENTS

◙

List of Illustrations　vii

Acknowledgments　xi

CHAPTER ONE　1
Introduction

CHAPTER TWO　13
The Moving Image in the Nineteenth Century

CHAPTER THREE　27
Approaching Cinema: The Chronophotographers

CHAPTER FOUR　57
The Search for a Material: The Development of Celluloid

CHAPTER FIVE　79
Shaping the Future: Thomas Alva Edison and the Kinetoscope

CHAPTER SIX　103
Seeking an Answer: Out of the Lantern Tradition

CHAPTER SEVEN　133
Multiple Questions: The Many Cinemas of 1896–1900

Bibliography　165

Index　179

LIST OF
ILLUSTRATIONS

▣

FIGURE 1. The Kineoptoscope projector   7

FIGURE 2. Two forms of the second model Theatrograph   9
projector of Robert William Paul from 1896

FIGURE 3. A pair of side-by-side dissolving view lanterns,   16
as used at the Royal Polytechnic Institution, London, in
1843

FIGURE 4. Five moving slides for the magic lantern   18

FIGURE 5. The Phenakistoscope in use before a mirror   20

FIGURE 6. Emile Reynaud's Praxinoscope Theater of 1879   22

FIGURE 7. The Théâtre Optique of Emile Reynaud in use   23

FIGURE 8. The Astronomical Revolver of Jules Janssen,   30
photographing an eclipse of the sun in 1874

FIGURE 9. Leland Stanford's horse Sallie Gardner, pho-   33
tographed at the gallop by Eadweard Muybridge in 1878

FIGURE 10. The Photographic Gun of Étienne-Jules   37
Marey, 1882

FIGURE 11. The second model of the Schnellseher, some-   45
times called the Electrical Tachyscope, of Ottomar
Anschütz, as illustrated by *Scientific American* in 1889

FIGURE 12. The 60 mm film camera of Georges Demenÿ,   53
first model, 1893

FIGURE 13. The emulsion-mixing room at the Lumière   73
factory in Lyon, 1894

FIGURE 14. The production model of the Kinetoscope   87
viewer of Thomas Edison and William Kennedy Laurie
Dickson, 1894

FIGURE 15. An early model Mutoscope of Herman   95
Casler, from 1897

FIGURE 16. Two versions of Robert Dempsey Gray's   111
apparatus of 1895

FIGURE 17. The Bioscop double-band projector of Max   114
Skladanowsky, 1895

FIGURE 18. The Phantoscope of Charles Francis Jenkins   122
and Thomas Armat, from their patent applied for on
August 28, 1895, and issued July 20, 1897

FIGURE 19. The Lumière Cinématographe set up for use   130
as a camera, from an 1896 engraving

FIGURE 20. The Lumière Cinématographe in use as a   137
projector, from an 1896 engraving

FIGURE 21. The second model of the Theatrograph pro-   141
jector of Robert William Paul

FIGURE 22. Four intermittent movements   145

FIGURE 23. The Lumière Kinora as it was originally pro-   149
posed in the patent of 1896

FIGURE 24. The Street Cinematograph of W. C. Hughes,   154
from an 1898 illustration

FIGURE 25. The Docwra triple lantern of 1888, designed   156
by Colin Docwra and made by W. C. Hughes of London

ACKNOWLEDGMENTS

No one who works in early cinema works alone. If, like an archaeologist, every scholar has her or his own "dig," where research into a particular topic demands close attention to the records of a single town, individual, or company, then the interpretation of the shards recovered from that dig instantly requires collegial exchange with a wide network of scholarship from both past and present. I am particularly grateful for the monumental works of many scholars of the past, including Henry Hopwood, Karl Forch, F. Paul Liesegang, Gordon Hendricks, and Hermann Hecht, to name only a few from a long list; I am in awe of their persistence and thoroughness, and their thoughtful contributions to a field that in their own times must have been considered even more unlikely than it sometimes seems to be today. In my own work, I have been the grateful recipient of strong encouragement, shared materials, generous explanations, puzzling questions, and thoughtful insights from Michelle Aubert, John and Bill Barnes, Stephen Bottomore, Marta Braun, Sid Brooks, Richard Brown, Mervyn Heard, Stephen Herbert, Cornelia Kemp, Frank Kessler, Paul Kusters, Hauke Lange-Fuchs, Sabine Lenk, Martin Loiperdinger, Laurent Mannoni, Luke McKernan, Corinna Müller, Pamela Müller, Charles Musser, Keld Nielsen, Aurelio de los Reyes, Lester Smith, Virgilio Tosi, Vanessa Toulmin, and many others; I thank them all for their time and trouble, for shared research and joyous meetings.

It has been my intention from the start of this book to dedicate it to Anette Schroeder, without whose practical, emo-

tional, and intellectual support it would not have been possible
to begin, much less to finish. But with her kind permission, I
must now expand this dedication, for in the intervening months
two great cineastes have passed away, both friends and gentlemen in very different ways, and to both of whom I would dearly
have loved to have shown this completed work: John Gillett and
David Shipman. Neither was an early cinema specialist; both
were, uniquely, specialists in the whole of cinema, incorporating its widest ranges into their lives, and dedicated to passing
their extraordinary knowledge on to others through both gra-
cious writings and eloquent public programs. In the early 1970s,
François Truffaut once told me that he thought it was no longer
possible to do what he had done two decades earlier: to be
engaged with every kind of film, see everything, write about
everything. The cinema had become too big, he said, it was now
a time for specialists. John Gillett and David Shipman were the
necessary exceptions that proved Truffaut correct. They went to
every movie, they burrowed through archives after surviving
pictures from the past, and they were engaged with the whole of
the cinema. In another land they would have been living
national treasures; we are all the poorer for their absence.

CHAPTER ONE

□

Introduction

"Edison or Lumière?" was the headline of an article published in the German showman's magazine *Der Komet*, on September 26, 1896. Written by Theodore Bläser, by the date of the article himself an exhibitor, filmmaker, and sales agent for projectors made by Otto Thiele in Geneva, his article contended that Thomas Edison was the real inventor of the new "wonder apparatus" and that the Lumière brothers had merely followed up Edison's invention of the Kinetoscope and turned it into a projection device. The fight over who was the "true" inventor of the cinema had begun, a battle that would last through a century of scholarship, cause many distortions of the historical record, and quickly come to involve issues of national pride and politics.

By the 1930s, several inventors had become fixed in their respective national pantheons as the "true" originator of motion pictures: in America, Thomas Alva Edison; in France, Louis and Auguste Lumière; in Germany, Max Skladanowsky; in Britain, William Friese Greene. At the same time, lively debates were underway on behalf of other inventors whose advocates contended that they had been overlooked as the movies became a worldwide industry and that their contributions as the "true" discoverers of the cinema had been obscured: C. Francis Jenkins, Thomas Armat, and the Latham family (America); Étienne-Jules Marey (France); Oskar Messter (Germany); and Robert William Paul (Britain).

1

There was never a shortage of candidates for the role of movie inventor (Austria could point to Theodor Reich, Poland to Kasimierz Proszynski, Russia to Ivan Akimovich Akimov), and later research that clarified the work of many of these pioneers seemed at the same time to create another byzantine layer of claims and counterclaims, as the details of the contributions of another whole group of inventors and mechanics was brought into the foreground of the historical record, among them Edison's assistant William Kennedy Laurie Dickson in America, Marey's assistant Georges Demenÿ in France, and Paul's one-time collaborator Birt Acres in England.

Recent writers on the origins of the cinema have tended to avoid many of the most egregious battles of the past and, while telling the story of the first experiments that led to moving pictures in some detail, have suggested that the cinema came to life through the near-simultaneous and independent efforts of many inventors in several countries. If this formulation avoids the sticky problem of naming the "first" inventor, it shares with earlier historical writings an implicitly linear concept of the discovery, introduction, and dissemination of moving pictures just before the turn of the century. The year 1895 is packed with crucial developments in film history, many with clear precedents reaching back over the previous decade, and the six months from November 1895 through April 1896 found moving pictures commercially shown to public audiences and specialist scientific groups in dozens of countries around the world. Getting the chronology of this period sorted out, understanding the mostly Greek- or Latin-based terminology that the inventors affixed to their new devices, and comprehending the relative contributions of the scores of figures involved in the story are together a powerful urge toward a careful linear exposition of the period. Yet a linear approach does not serve the material well: the work of some figures is unbalanced to make it fit the development scheme, other figures are omitted for the sake of neatness, and flattening the image of the period leads to oversimplification and a weakening of the relationships between various participants, denying the robust energy of the era.

Implicit in a linear search for "firsts" is the the question "'First' of what?" The habitual and often unconscious answer to this question projects backward in time the later characteristics of "the movies" drawn from an era well after the period of invention and exploration. This later concept of "the movies" came only with a matured technology and an established business practice that bears little or no relationship to the emerging medium of the 1890s. The beginning *was* the beginning, and few if any of its initial participants had any idea of the scope and impact that the new medium would have in the following century.

Whether this retrospective reading of a stabilized medium into its origins is represented by a search for the first close-up—or the first piece of edited film—as an indication of the origins of film language, or by the quest for the first use of the Maltese cross for giving intermittent movement to the film band in mechanical apparatus, the beginning of moving pictures is retrospectively defined by a context, style, technology, and presentational apparatus that became an emerging practice only after 1900 and stabilized in the next decade. While this search for early examples of either aesthetic or mechanical practice in the cinema is a useful historical endeavor in relation to later developments, it does not adequately reflect the activity of the 1890s, and in preselecting and prevaluing only some developments in the period of invention it begs the question of why certain artifacts, business proceedures, and film subjects were "successful" and others "failed."

The present book is a first attempt to examine the early days of moving pictures from a nonlinear and multidirectional perspective. It attempts to view the birth of moving pictures without privileging later developments from outside the period. While it is broadly organized chronologically, it strongly contends that not only were moving picture entertainments as they have been known throughout the twentieth century invented during this period (movies on celluloid, with a Maltese cross intermittent movement, seen by large audiences in fixed theaters, purveyed as storytelling entertainment or factual record), but also that several other kinds of moving picture were invented as well. It is these alternative proposals for moving pictures—as family portraits, as an instrument of science, as a mechanical variety act, as stereoscopic photography—that make the decade of the 1890s so diverse in its inventions and so resistant to attempts to force its artifacts into a single line of development leading only to the mass entertainment medium of the twentieth century.

These alternative ideas about moving pictures, about their uses and properties, directly influenced the many technological solutions to the problem of capturing and reproducing motion through photography, and account for the plethora of mechanical and optical apparatus that appeared in the 1890s. For there was no single predetermined and inevitable technical solution to the reproduction of movement for projection on a screen. Many technological solutions were possible—moving pictures on glass plates or on celluloid, with intermittent movement or without—and many were tried. Frequently, the relative success or failure of these alternative solutions is a retrospective judgment made possible only by the later stablilization of the technology within a single social apparatus of exhibition on celluloid in large theaters before mass audiences. To the inventors, showmen, filmmakers, and manufacturers of the late nineteenth century, this particular later resolution of the medium was only one of several possible results of their work, and a consequence that few imagined with any clarity.

This study of the beginnings of the cinema up to 1900 has been heavily influenced by recent writing about the history of technology, especially the work of scholars interested in the social construction of technology. Their work recognizes the influence of a variety of social groups on technology, not only in determining its use and development, but also in influencing the technical design of the artifact itself. The first generation of movie inventors came from a variety of backgrounds, including optics, magic lantern work, photography, scientific research, magic, and electrical manufacture. They lived in a fast-changing era that was characterized by a multiplicity of competing solutions to technological problems. One illustration of multiple solutions to a technical issue is well exemplified in the long process of establishing electrical power generating and distributing systems. As late as 1913, for example, public electrical supply in greater London was provided by 65 separate electrical utilities with 70 generating stations using 49 different types of supply systems on 10 different frequencies, with 32 voltage levels for the transmission of electrical power and 24 for its distribution (Hughes 1983, 227). The rapid and confusing spread of competing electrical systems and the earlier rapid and intensive development of telegraphic communications frame an era that also saw the phonograph begin to replace music boxes in the home, the spread of photography to a mass market, the use of X-rays in medical diagnosis, and experiments with gliders and advanced balloons leading to powered flight. Within this changing world, the first generation of moving picture inventors approached the problems of capturing and recreating natural motion through photography. Their respective experiences and habits of thinking influenced both their concepts of what moving pictures could be, and the specific artifacts they created to fulfil their dreams.

Social influences on the development of technical apparatus are not limited solely to inventors, mechanics, and builders; influence was also exerted through the varying experiences of exhibitors, audiences, officials, and a variety of other social groups, or by exceptional events, contemporary theories and practices, existing social patterns, and problem-solving habits. The exhibition of moving pictures in a large variété or vaudeville theater in a major city, for example, made demands on the construction of mechanical equipment and its source of illumination that were distinctively different from those required by an itinerant single showman renting storefront spaces in small towns, or exhibiting in hotel and public house venues.

The most useful model of the multiple influences that shape a technological artifact has been suggested by Wiebe E. Bijker in his description of the "technological frame." His model should be "understood as a frame with respect to technology, rather than as the technologist's frame" (Bijker 1987, 172). As such, it is intended to apply not just to groups of inventors, mechanics, and engineers directly involved in applying their skills to an artifact, but also to all social groups who had any involvement with the artifact and who as a consequence influenced the artifact, whether as users, sellers, regulators, observers, or paying customers. Moreover, Bijker explicitly intends the technological frame as a construct "intended to apply to the *interaction* of various actors. Thus it is not an individual's characteristic, nor the characteristic of systems or institutions; frames are located *between* actors, not *in* actors or *above* actors" (1987, 172). The members of a social group attribute various meanings to a technological artifact and in so doing provide an understanding and shared meaning for the artifact, or in Bijker's words, "as it were, a grammar for it" (1987, 173). Various actors or social groups can also have stronger or weaker identifications with a particular technological frame that can additionally determine the degree of their inclusiveness within that frame, and their consequent response to an artifact and their vision for its use.

One example of how a technological frame can be used to illuminate problems in the early history of the cinema can be seen from a brief look at a few of the figures associated with the technological frame including magic lantern work (discussed in more detail in chapter 6). As an important predecessor of the cinema, with its own tradition of "moving" pictures and visual storytelling, its own exhibition patterns and manufacturers of optical apparatus, magic lantern work had an immense influence on the first years of the cinema. The English inventor Robert W. Paul declared that his first projection apparatus was intended "to be capable of attachment to any existing lantern" (Paul 1936, 43), just as Cecil Wray's first apparatus of 1896 was a simple projection mechanism intended to fit wholly within the standard slide stage of a normal magic lantern (Wray, 1896). Both machines were quickly taken up by exhibitors with magic lantern backgrounds, and Wray's device was purchased and marketed by Riley Brothers of Bradford, England, a well-known firm of lantern and slide manufacturers, as Riley's Kineoptoscope.

Paul was an electrical engineer whose firm manufactured instruments for the growing electrical industry, and whose first contact with film came through the manufacture of reproduction Edison Kinetoscopes; notwithstanding his 1936 statement about the practical dimensions of his first film projector, his degree of inclusion in a technological frame of magic lantern work can be considered small. With the wider contacts of his electrical manufacturing business, his apparatus was taken up quickly not only by lanternists, but also by magicians and travelling showmen, ultimately directly influencing Georges Méliès in France and Oskar Messter in Germany, among many others. Cecil Wray was also an electrical engineer by trade, and also took up film work through the Edison Kinetoscope, patenting a

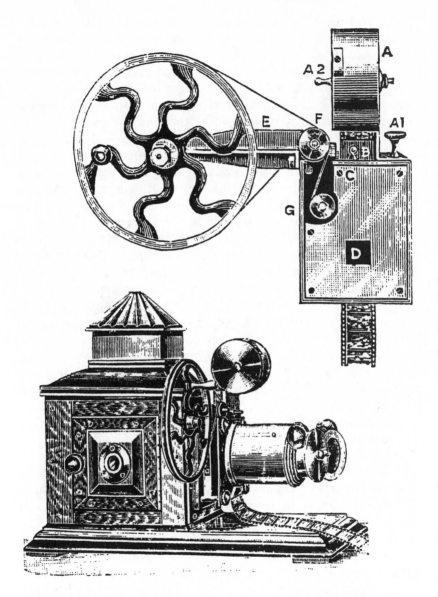

FIGURE 1. The Kineoptoscope projector, patented by Cecil Wray in August, 1896, and manufactured by Riley Brothers of Bradford in 1897, which fit into the slide stage of a normal magic lantern. Above, a front view of the compact apparatus; below, the Kineoptoscope mounted in a magic lantern.

device to turn it into a projection apparatus of dubious workability in January 1895 (Wray 1895). By making a film projector
that would fit within a standard magic lantern slide stage, using
the lantern's own light source and optics, and selling his patent
in spring 1896 to an established magic lantern business, Wray
demonstrated his more substantive inclusion in a technological
frame of magic lantern work as he thought of moving pictures
as a new accessory for the lantern. Physically and technically
limited to an existence wholly within existing patterns of magic
lantern work, his Kineoptoscope, although popular and widely
used in smaller venues in the United Kingdom, remained a
regional device and did not have an impact on the emerging new
medium in any way comparable to the international reach of
Paul's Theatrograph. Within months Wray moved away from his
early commitment to the lantern, designing a new apparatus
that was not tied to the lantern slide stage, and a year later his
third device was largely independent of these roots.

A figure with a high inclusion in a technological frame of
magic lantern work was Max Skladanowsky in Berlin. He toured
with his father and older brother Emil giving dissolving magic
lantern shows from 1879; his Bioscop moving picture projection
device was wholly derived from dissolving lantern practice, projecting alternate frames from two intermittently moving bands
of celluloid film (discussed in chapter 6). His degree of inclusion
in this frame (and his simultaneous inclusion in a technological
frame of mechanical varieté showmen) was so high that he had
a limited vision of moving pictures as an independent entity,
and once he had travelled with his Bioscop double-projector
through many of the same venues in Scandinavia and northern
Germany that were the sites of his previous lantern and
mechanical varieté act appearances, he saw little further utility
in his invention.

By illuminating the interactions of figures around an artifact, a technological frame can explain how the environment
structures an artifact's design, as was the case for both Paul and
Wray, whose machines could instantly enter a market established by magic lantern work. But Wray's Kineoptoscope was
designed and marketed wholly within magic lantern practice,
unlike Paul's Theatrograph, so it was Paul's machine that broke
quickly away from the lantern world and became the second

most widely used device across Europe (after the Lumière Ciné-matographe). Skladanowsky's Bioscop was useful to its maker-exhibitor—he and his brother had previously travelled with a self-made mechanical theater—but was not readily trans-portable or replicable for other showmen lacking their particu-lar skills, experience, and dedication to the unwieldy apparatus: by the time Skladanowsky gave his last performance in March 1897, with the Bioscop II single-band film projector, events had moved decisively past him and his horizon limited to thinking of his invention as just another mechanical varieté act.

A technological frame can also explain how an artifact itself structures the social environment in which it operates. Through the end of 1896, both the London magician David Devant and the Berlin operator Karl Pahl recall giving private film showings in the homes of wealthy residents (Barnes 1976, 118; Pahl 1933, 4), continuing a long tradition of private perfor-

FIGURE 2. Two forms of the second model Theatrograph projector of Robert William Paul from 1896: on the left, the apparatus is mounted on a strong iron stand for use in theaters, and on the right it sits on top of a transportable case used by travelling exhibitors.

mances by magic lantern showmen. The new "wonder apparatus" was also frequently exhibited at upper-class charity events
or as a special attraction at middle-class entertainments, such as
the summer 1896 Proms concerts in London and the concerts
and lectures at Unity Hall in Hartford, Connecticut (Rossell
1995, 210; Musser 1990, 140). After the worldwide publicity
given the shocking fire at the Société Charité Maternelle in
Paris in March 1897, in which 143 French socialites died,
reports of private home screenings or upper-class venues outside
strictly theatrical settings are almost nonexistent. The highly
flammable celluloid that was an integral part of many moving
picture shows meant that some social groups quickly decided to
avoid involvement with the new medium. An apparatus that to
lanternists was an exciting addition to their repertoire was seen
by others as a danger to public safety. These conflicting views of
different social groups shaped both the location and the acceptance of the new medium; it was to overcome such conflicts
that inventors proposed the variety of alternative technologies
that characterize the beginnings of the cinema. Officials in
many localities had already regulated the lantern showman's
choice of illumination for projection, defining the use of oil
lamps, coal gas, oxy-hydrogen limelight, oxygen-ether limelight,
or electricity for magic lantern shows, but the authorities took
a new look at their licensing procedures for moving picture presentations, which quickly had a direct influence on an
exhibitor's choice of location and conditions of exhibition. As
interaction within this technological frame built up around the
artifacts of cinema, and stable social groups continued to exert
their influences on it, some technical options rapidly withered
away while others grew in importance. Many of the alternative
technologies proposed for moving pictures were a direct
response to this characteristic of celluloid movies, and were
attempts to bring the sensational new attraction to groups who
rejected the dangers of celluloid.

A nonlinear approach to the early history of the cinema
accounts for many seemingly conflicting and contradictory
developments of the period. In November 1896, when Pierre-
Victor Continsouza and René Bünzli patented a new apparatus
that substituted a glass plate for the celluloid film band used in
other projectors, and predicted the end of celluloid film strip

moving pictures, they were not simply proposing another wild device for producing moving pictures (Continsouza and Bünzli 1896). Nor were they just trying to avoid prior patents from other inventors: they envisioned an alternative cinema using nonflammable materials that would be located in the home and be shown to small groups, one that relied on the substantial experience of contemporary photographers in working with glass plates. As later taken up by Leonard Ulrich Kamm, G. Bettini, and others (see chapter 7), such an alternative cinema was not at all out of the question at a time when the normal picture size of a public projection was frequently about three feet in width, or at most four feet, and neither the technology nor the business practices of the cinema had yet stabilized. The proposal of Continsouza and Bünzli is only one reminder that, in Bijker's words, "an historical account founded on the retrospective success of an artifact leaves much untold" (Bijker 1987, 24).

By examining the artifacts of the period symmetrically, that is, looking with equal interest at both "successful" and "failed" artifacts, retrospective distortion of the historical record can be avoided. Symmetrical consideration of the artifacts also rejects the technological determinism in which there is only one "right" solution to a technological problem. It is clear from the early days of moving pictures that there were many possible options of reaching the goal of projected moving pictures, including mechanical and optical intermittent systems, glass and celluloid image carriers, and direct or indirect projections for enlargement. Some of these alternatives provided strikingly superior features to the "successful" technology that has been privileged in most writing about the period. By searching only for predetermined elements of the later, stabilized technology, in particular celluloid film bands and the Maltese cross intermittent movement, assuming that these elements were the sole necessary and inevitable components of the medium, or the technologically "correct" solution, the success of that technology becomes self-justifying, giving no real explanation for its survival. Moveover, there were powerful precinema examples of nonmechanical intermittent movements that produced viable moving pictures, particularly in the Praxinoscope and in the public success of Émile Renaud's Théâtre Optique (see chapter 2) that was based on it. Between 1895 and 1910 over 200 patents in America, France, Germany, and England proposed elements of optical projection systems. Optical systems with continuously running film solved the severe early problems of scratching and tearing the flimsy celluloid band, as well as reducing the irritating flicker of light on the screen that frequently plagued early exhibitions. That these optical solutions were not just a theoretical alternative is exemplified by the later development of the Mechau projector of 1912–34, of which more than 500 examples were made and which proved not only an excellent theatrical projector but also had a revival after 1945 in television work since it was especially well suited to originating film broadcasts. Mechanical intermittents, then, were hardly inevitable, yet technological, social, and economic interests converged to make this the preferred solution.

The several kinds of cinemas that are present in the early days of moving pictures provide a context against which answers to questions about the beginnings of twentieth-century moving picture culture can begin to be approached. The present multidirectional approach to the invention of the movies recognizes that in the beginning very few of its inventors had a vision of what moving pictures might become, or of just what course they might take in developing into a lasting medium. It provides a window on a tumultous, energetic, inventive, and exciting period of history that has long been hidden by extraneous—if sometimes entertaining—disputes both between inventors and between historians. Moving pictures appeared in many different countries at almost the same time; a near simultaneity of invention(s) typically produced by individuals or teams who "inferred from their familiarity with the state of the art the sites, figurative and literal, of critical-problem-solving activity and the nature of the problems" (Hughes 1983, 80). In the last decade of the nineteenth century, the state of the art in projection and visual storytelling was the magic lantern show, and it is with the world of the magic lantern exhibitor that the story of moving pictures begins.

CHAPTER TWO

The Moving Image
in the Nineteenth Century

By the second half of the nineteenth century, magic lantern exhibitions had become technologically sophisticated and visually refined productions. The introduction of dissolving views at the Royal Polytechnic Institution in London by Henry Langdon Childe in the early 1840s led to the development of at first double (biunial), then triple (triunial) lanterns capable of subtly blending one image into another, or producing a variety of effects from snow and rain to lightning and billowing smoke. One classic set of widely sold and used dissolving slides showed a pastoral scene, in full color, of a quiet country mill next to its still pond and surrounded by woodlands, its millwheel slowly turning in the late autumn sunlight. Slowly, a gentle snow began to fall; the the landscape was transformed into a bright winter day, with the pond frozen, the wheel still, and a family bundled in winter clothes scurrying down the path to the right of the pond. The scene then transformed again, into a lush green spring, fresh water turning the millwheel on a sparkling day; then a family of swans paddled into view across the the pond, unexpectedly pausing to bend their elegant necks to feed beneath the surface of the water. The apparatus required to exhibit this set of dissolving views was not especially elaborate; its effects could be manipulated by any experienced lanternist. It could be purchased or rented from dozens of suppliers in a range of qualities, determined by the caliber of the glass painting in the set. Its placement in an evening's program might well be set off by the showing of hand-cranked chromatrope slides, also invented by Childe, where abstract painted designs gave a spectacular effect of both depth and motion comparable to looking at the geometrical patterns of a kaleidoscope.

The effects of *The Old Mill* were provided by a combination of rackwork and slipping slides. The basic scene used two glass slides sandwiched together, with the background scene painted on one glass and the millwheel on a separate rotating glass disk mounted in a geared frame that was set in motion by a small crank in the side of the slide's frame. Another geared rackwork slide provided the snowfall for this or any other appropriate image, while the pedestrians and swans were moved across the landscape by levers on their own shards of painted glass in slipping slides. The overall effect of the set was a combination of the quality and precision of the painting on the slides, and the artistic skills of the lanternist were crucial in manipulating the apparatus, dissolving from one view to the next by either adjusting the illumination or by moving a blending shutter in front of the lantern's lenses while at the same time cranking the rackwork handle or tugging at the levers. Other popular dissolving views included the eruption of Mount Vesuvius, St. Paul's Church in London with the effects of a rainbow, historical scenes of battles and ships in harbor, and a variety of Romantic legends, from the tomb of Abelard and Heloise to the ruins of old abbeys and castles.

At London's Royal Polytechnic Institution, like the Eden Musee in New York one of the established centers of lantern exhibitions intended for both instruction and entertainment, a battery of giant lanterns using elaborately painted slides as large as 8½ inches wide and 6½ inches high and served by a team of operators provided even more elaborate shows. *The Optical Magic Lantern Journal* reported on one new production in 1894, *Gabriel Grubb*, painted by W. R. Hill, a former apprentice to Childe, in which the story's churchyard scene alone required one view and fifteen effects:

> There are goblins coming out of graves, leaping over tombstones, streaming out of windows, standing on their heads

and sinking into the ground. Illumination of windows and clock faces. Gabriel himself in a number of different positions of surprise and terror, and at the close of the scene the whole picture moves, and we appear to travel down through the earth to the goblins' cave, passing through the various strata of unmentionable objects such as we might expect to find in churchyard mould. In the same set Mr. Hill also introduced a panorama, the glass of which is 38 inches by 8 inches, illustrating Gabriel's walk from the village to the old abbey church. (Barnes 1985, 4)

A panorama slide from *Gabriel Grubb* measuring more than three feet in length is preserved at the Cinémathèque française.

Many professional touring lanternists painted their own slides, and the quality can frequently be astonishing. The reputation of a lanternist depended as much on the merit of his brushwork and visual interpretation as on an ability to manipulate special effects in the lantern. The travelling lecturer and showman Paul Hoffmann toured the capitals of central Europe giving talks on themes as diverse as "Polar Expeditions from 1845 to 1859," "A Trip through Central Africa," and "Earthquakes, Volcanoes, and the Destruction of Pompeii." Over half of the seventy-one slides in his presentation of "The Divine Comedy of Dante Alighieri" were modelled on the engravings of Gustave Doré, and for a presentation of "The Niebelungenring" forty-four surviving slides were painted from the original stage designs commissioned by Richard Wagner for the first complete cycle of his operas at Bayreuth (Hoffmann and Junker 1982). Other sources for Hoffmann's slides included illustrated scientific works on geology and astronomy, woodcuts by the painter Friedrich Preller, and the watercolors of English architect T. W. Atkinson. At the same time, Hoffmann's erudite shows capitalized on the current interests of his audiences: he launched his Dante program in 1868, three years after the Europewide celebrations of the poet's 600th anniversary, and his Wagner program in 1876, the year the Festspielhaus in Bayreuth was completed and the presentation there of the complete cycle of Wagner's four operas became a national event.

The images produced on the screen by Hoffmann's slides, now preserved at the Historisches Museum in Frankfurt, and by those in use at the Polytechnic institution in London, the Eden Musee in New York, and by many professional lanternists were rock-steady, clear, and subtle pictures superior to those in the illustrated books of the day and often comparable to the genre paintings, woodcuts, and engravings that could be seen in gal-

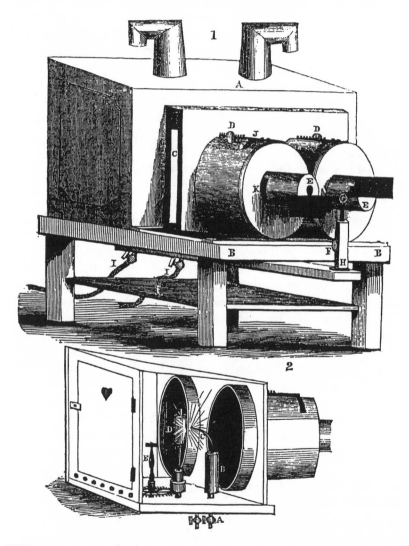

FIGURE 3. A pair of side-by-side dissolving view lanterns as used at the Royal Polytechnic Institution, London, in 1843.

leries and museums. They bore little resemblance to the flickering, blurred, and frequently scratched black-and-white offerings of the first celluloid moving pictures. For a decade after film projection swept the world in 1896, many critics lamented the public enthusiasm for what they saw as a distinctly inferior medium. Cecil Hepworth, a lanternist and son of a lanternist but in later years an outstanding British filmmaker, was heavily critical of the film image in 1896, decrying the "animated palsyscopes" and questioning how long it would be before the public "gets tired of the uncomfortably jerky photographs. Living photographs are about as far from being things of beauty as anything possibly could be" (Bottomore 1996, 137).

Along with high-quality painted slides and cheaper color-lithographed or transfer slides widely sold to a mass market after about 1870, mechanical moving slides were also an important part of the magic lantern repertoire. The earliest seem to have been produced in at least 1697, when the Jena physicist Erhard Weigel made slides of "goats butting, and a bear rising and attacking with his paws a man dressed in a Swiss outfit" (Lange-Fuchs 1995a, 14); Pieter van Musschenbroek, a professor of natural philosophy and mathematics at Utrecht, published illustrations of five moving slides, including four different lever slides and a hand-cranked windmill slide in his *Essais de physique* in 1739.

But from about 1866, with the introduction of the Choreutoscope by J. Beale, an engineer in Greenwich, England, a new kind of movement entered lantern shows. In the Choreutoscope, a version of which was also patented by O. B. Brown in 1869 in the United States, a disk with images of sequenced movement was rotated intermittently by a pin-and-slot gearing similar to a Maltese cross, with a slotted shutter rotated synchronously in front of the lantern's lens. The interchangeable disks held painted representations of tumblers or dancers, and in use gave the impression of continuous movement on the screen. This lantern accessory, popularized by the lantern maker James Henry Steward in London and improved in 1884 by William Charles Hughes in his Giant Choreutoscope, melded nineteenth-century persistence of vision devices with magic lantern projection: "The object of my invention," wrote Brown of his device, "is to combine the principle of the phan-

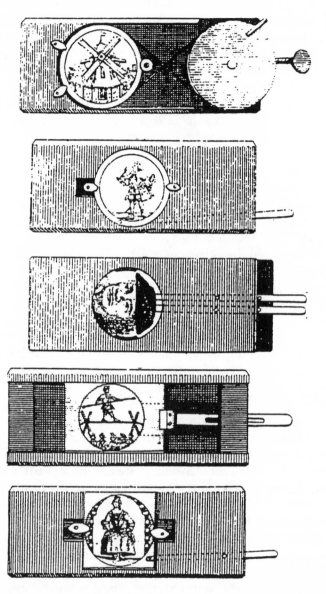

FIGURE 4. Five moving slides for the magic lantern. Top to bottom: the windmill sails revolve, a man drinks, a man rolls his eyes, a tightrope walker moves across his rope, and a woman jumps. From Pieter van Musschenbroek, *Essais de physique*, 1739.

tasmascope, or phenakistoscope with that of the phantasmagoria, or magic-lantern, in an instrument . . . by means of which figures may be represented upon a wall or screen so as to produce the appearance of objects in motion" (Brown 1869, 1).

The Phenakistoscope had been a popular toy for three decades when it was adapted for projection. A disk of heavy paper with printed sequences of drawn movement separated by slots around its circumference, when it was held with the printed side towards a mirror and spun, a viewer looking through the slots at the image reflected in the mirror saw figures of men playing leapfrog or a bouncing ball in continuous, if repetitive, motion. The near-simultaneous invention of Simon Stampfer in Austria in December 1832, who called it a "stroboscopic disk," and of Joseph Plateau in Belgium in January 1833, versions of the Phenakistoscope were marketed in Germany, Austria, France, and England by mid-1833.

An improvement on the Phenakistoscope was suggested the same year by Stampfer and in 1834 by William George Horner in England, where the images were painted on a long band that was placed inside a deep cylinder with a slotted top; looking at the band through the slots when the cylinder was spun produced the same effect of movement without requiring a mirror. This device, named the Zoetrope, was widely manufactured and sold from the mid-1860s, when new patents for it appeared in both America and Europe (Hallett, 1867; May 1867; Lincoln 1867).

The Phenakistoscope and the Zoetrope both relied on the nineteenth-century concept of "persistence of vision," where it was thought that a still image was retained briefly on the human retina so that if more than about sixteen impressions per second of phased movement were received by the eye, it could not discriminate between them. The eye, therefore, perceived the separate drawings (later, photographs) as continuous movement. This idea of the persistence of vision is an incorrect description of the physiological process of how the rods and cones in the retina actually perceive and digest motion (see Chanan 1996, 54–69), but it is still a useful guideline to the mechanical thresholds necessary for the reproduction of movement in nineteenth-century devices and, later, in celluloid movies. Just as Newtonian physics is a functional description of

FIGURE 5. The Phenakistoscope in use before a mirror.

the immediate world that has been superceded by Einstein's theory of relativity and the quantum mechanics of Niels Bohr, the practical threshold described by the concept of the persistence of vision serves as a fully adequate description of the physical requirements of any mechanical instrument intended to reproduce motion for a human observer.

An ingenious improvement in the stroboscopic replication of movement was patented by the Frenchman Emile Reynaud in 1877. His Praxinoscope was a shallow drum fitted around its inside circumference with a drawn band of images similar to those used in the Zoetrope, gaining its intermittency from a faceted cylinder at the center of the drum fitted with small mirrors (Reynaud 1877). His delightfully whimsical chromolithographs of a young girl skipping rope or catching fish from a tank provided clear and vivid movements for a viewer watching reflections of the band in the spinning mirrors, and by 1879 he had packaged his device as the Praxinoscope Theater, where the movements from the spinning mirrors were seen through a tiny proscenium as if they appeared on a stage.

More elaborate versions of Reynaud's apparatus used a toy steam engine or a primitive electric motor to rotate the drum. In 1888 Reynaud created his ultimate moving picture machine, the Théâtre Optique. This was a giant-sized projecting Praxinoscope where mirrors reflected his drawn images through a lens onto a small overhead screen, which was supplied with background scenery by a separate magic lantern (Reynaud 1888). The drawings of sequenced movement for the Théâtre Optique were made on a flexible band 65 mm wide with sprocket holes reinforced with metal ringlets to give secure positioning to the band as it moved through the device by means of two large hand cranks; a typical band held about 700 images on a band 45–50 meters long. With this apparatus, Reynaud opened a show of living pictures at the Cabinet Fantastique of the Musée Grevin in Montmartre, Paris, on October 28, 1892, giving over 12,800 performances that were seen by half a million visitors through 1900. With the accompaniment of a piano player and a singer, Reynaud narrated the story of his band of drawings as he manipulated the images backward and forward through the Théâtre Optique in a performance lasting about fifteen minutes.

FIGURE 6. Emile Reynaud's Praxinoscope Theater of 1879.

FIGURE 7. The Théâtre Optique of Emile Reynaud in use. The magic lantern D at left projected a background scene, while a second lantern B at center right illuminated Reynaud's painted band of figures, which were projected through the lens C at center and reflected from the mirror M at upper left and combined with the background on the screen E.

The introduction of photographic images to magic lantern practice occurred only shortly after the invention of photography when the brothers Frederick and William Langenheim of Philadelphia offered their Hyalotype slides for sale in 1849. Produced on glass by an albumen process, they offered views of historic buildings in Philadelphia, Washington, D.C., and New York, as well as portraits of famous Americans. The use of photographic slides spread rapidly, not only due to the interest in the new process and their fine reproduction of detail, but also from the introduction of a new type of magic lantern by Lorenzo J. Marcy of Philadelphia called the Sciopticon. Equipped with a new type of lamp burning paraffin or kerosene and using two separately adjustable wicks, the Sciopticon featured an excellent set of lenses and condensers modelled on the Petzval portrait lens, yet was relatively inexpensive. The combination of excellent optics with a much brighter source of illumination meant that photographic slides were shown to great advantage, and all but the most exquisitely made hand-painted slides showed their flaws on the screen. As manufacturers produced more and more Sciopticon-type lanterns for general use, photographic slides became increasingly popular and were made in large numbers for either sale or rental.

By 1878 photographic slide sets were produced in "life model" series, in which actors were posed in stage settings representing the various scenes of a narrative story drawn from popular literature, songs, or plays. The English firm of York and Son were specialists in life model series, as were Bamforth's in Yorkshire and the American lecturer Alexander Black, who opened a full-length fiction play called *Miss Jerry* in New York City in late 1894 using posed slides taken in both exterior and interior locations. But most life model slides were taken in the secure environment of a studio, and Bamforth, for example, had a completely outfitted glass-roofed facility at their premises, surviving photographs of which show painted backdrops, stored flats, props, and an open foreground playing area that is indistinguishable from the appearance of many early movie stages.

Most photographic slides were offered in series of anywhere from 15 to 125 slides, and by the 1890s the catalogs of major suppliers in America and Europe frequently ran to 300 pages and hundreds of individual sets. It is no accident that the categories in which these slide sets were offered are the same categories with which early celluloid films were described, as illustrated by the eleven divisions of the York and Son catalog: Travel, Science and Education, War, Religious and Moral, Temperance, Pathetic, Comic, Fairy Tales, Mechanical Effects, Illustrated Songs, Miscellaneous. Travel sets and comic sets were the most prevalent in the York catalog, representing about half of their offerings (Henry 1984, 13), an emphasis replicated as well by the earliest filmmakers. Photographic slides issued in thematic sets were the basic stock used for magic lantern programs at the end of the nineteenth century. In the same era, the development of faster photographic plates and new types of shutters helped photographers capture moving subjects with unprecedented clarity. These artists and scientists who froze time in their cameras took the first decisive steps toward photographic moving pictures, and their specialized work was called chronophotography.

CHAPTER THREE

Approaching Cinema:
The Chronophotographers

The cinema's closest relative at the end of the nineteenth century, so close as to be indistinguishable in many ways from the very first movie presentations in both content and conception, was the specialized branch of photography known as chronophotography. Its three major figures were Eadweard Muybridge, a photographer of Western landscapes, who made the first instantaneous series photographs in 1878 and then promoted his method in lectures across America and Europe; Étienne-Jules Marey, a French physiologist, who devised many ingenious cameras for the scientific analysis of motion; and Ottomar Anschütz, a specialist in instant photography of animals in their natural settings, who ultimately created apparatus in the first half of the 1890s for viewing and projecting photographed motion.

Born in the laboratories of scientific researchers, chronophotography has two main branches: single-plate chronophotography, where multiple images of a moving object are recorded on a single photographic plate, and series photography, where single images of a subject in motion are recorded on a number of separate photographic plates. Series chronophotography is conceptually indistinguishable from a filmed motion picture, which consists of a long band of individually recorded still photographs, and both types of chronophotographic work made important contributions to the birth of the cinema. As a separate photographic specialty, chronophotography lasted only about twenty-five years before it was subsumed by the new medium of the cinema, or blended into the realm of scientific and industrial photography. Scientific chronophotography turned into a specialist branch of motion picture work using high-speed cameras and specially adapted films to analyze motion, and aesthetic chronophotography turned into the cinema itself, presenting the wonders of nature, famous leaders and celebrities of the day, and, ultimately, narrative stories to mass audiences throughout the world.

Along with its three outstanding practitioners, many others made contributions to developing chronophotography or used its specialized methods during its brief reign as the cutting edge of photographic work, among them Marey's assistant Georges Demenÿ, the physicist Ernst Mach, the gymnastics instructor Ernst Kohlrausch, the painter Thomas Eakins, and the medical researcher Albert Londe. One of the first was Bernhard Wilhelm Feddersen (1832–1918), who reflected images of a spark from a Leyden jar onto a photographic plate in 1858 so that he could measure the time-intervals of the jar's discharge as a part of his research into electricity (Feddersen 1858). This early use of photography to record a phenomenon the human eye could not discern and to measure the time intervals involved was possible only because the electrical spark was bright enough to leave a distinguishable impression on the slow photographic plates of the 1850s.

The concept of using a series of photographs with the phenakistiscope to recreate the impression of motion was widely discussed in the 1850s and 1860s, after it was first suggested by the Belgian scientist Joseph Plateau in 1849. The photographer A. François J. Claudet used a rotating plate-holder to take four pictures in rapid succession in 1852; Archibald Robinson increased this number to eight pictures in his camera of 1860; and Thomas Sutton suggested using multiple lenses and a rotating disk shutter in a camera to capture sequenced motion that same year (Liesegang 1926/1986, 30–31, 43). None of these experiments, or later proposals and apparatus by Charles Wheatstone, Jules Duboscq, Henry Cook, Gaetano Bonelli, Peter Henry Desvignes, and others, led to the actual production of chronophotographs that could be used to recreate the impression of motion: photographic emulsions were then too slow to allow the direct recording of any images other than posed movement. The few attempts to realize these early proposals used drawn images or, occasionally, individually posed photographic exposures. But the prescience and clear conceptual understanding by these pioneers of how movement could be captured photographically and then replayed later is strikingly illustrated in the comments of Louis Arthur Ducos du Hauron, who in 1864 applied for a patent for a multiple lens camera to take sequence photographs that could capture "the progress of a funeral procession, military reviews and manoeuvres, the vicissitudes of a battle, a public fête, a theatrical scene, the movements of one or more people, the play of expressions and, if one wished, the grimaces of a human face, etc., a marine view, the movements of waves, the movements of clouds in a stormy sky, particularly in a mountainous country, the eruption of a volcano, etc." (Coe 1992, 8).

A practical photographic device for making serial images of motion was used on December 8, 1874, by the French astronomer Pierre Jules César Janssen to record the transit of Venus across the sun during a solar eclipse. Janssen's "Révolver Astronomique" made a single exposure on the perimeter of an intermittently moved daguerreotype disk every seventy seconds, at one second intervals, producing forty-eight images on each of the four disks Janssen used that December day. A Maltese cross mechanism advanced the turning plate, and a revolving shutter with twelve slots rotated in front of the lens; the whole mechanism was operated by a clockwork motor. Janssen's resulting 192 images of the solar eclipse were possible only because of the intensity of the sun's light (which also accounts for the use of the anachronistic daguerreotype plate—a wet collodion plate was impractical in the device), and because the motion he recorded was slow, but Janssen suggested that his "photographic revolver" could take moving pictures of people and animals when photographic chemistry had progressed enough to allow pictures to be taken in shorter intervals of time.

Three years later, Janssen's predictions were realized through the energy, resourcefulness, and daring of Eadweard Muybridge, who created a sensation in the photographic world.

FIGURE 8. The Astronomical Revolver of Jules Janssen, photographing an eclipse of the sun in 1874. The sun's rays were directed to the apparatus by the mirror outside the building, and recorded on a circular daguerrotype plate rotated by a clockwork mechanism.

Born at Kingston, England, on April 9, 1830, Edward Muggeridge emigrated to the United States in 1851, changing his name to Eadweard Muybridge. He worked as a publisher's agent in New York City and then as a bookseller in California, where he began to take photographs (the best of several biographies is Haas 1976; for a brief survey, see Rossell 1996). He barely survived a dramatic stagecoach crash in Texas while on his way back to England in 1860, and during his recuperation in Kingston Muybridge learned wet-plate collodion photography, returning to America in 1866. The next year, he travelled widely across the West with a mobile photographic darkroom christened "The Flying Studio," and began to produce vivid landscapes and stereoscopic views under the pseudonym Helios. His growing reputation as a photographer led to an invitation in 1872 from Leland Stanford, an industrialist and former governor of California interested in horse racing, to use his skills with a camera to prove whether or not all four feet of a trotting horse are, or are not, off the ground at the same moment while the horse is at speed.

This question had been a matter of strong debate among sportsmen around the world, and an answer was important not only to racing trainers and riders, but also to scientists and physiologists with an interest in locomotion and to artists who represented the horse in motion in painting and sculpture. Muybridge's photographs of Stanford's famous trotting horse Occident were inconclusive, and he tried again in 1873 using the fastest wet-plate chemicals he could find; this second session produced a recognizable silhouette of the horse with all four feet off the ground at the same time.

Muybridge's work was now interrupted by another dramatic event: returning from a photographic trip in 1874, he discovered that his young wife had been made pregnant after an affair with Major Harry Larkyns, and Muybridge confronted Larkyns and shot him dead. His murder trial in San Francisco in February 1875 attracted national attention and was reported widely in the press; his subsequent acquittal on grounds of justifiable homicide increased his celebrity. Shortly after the end of the trial, Muybridge left the country on a long photographic trip to South America. During this period, the French physiologist Étienne-Jules Marey had published the first edition of *La Machine animal*

(Marey 1873), his ground-breaking report on animal locomotion that appeared in an English translation the next year (Marey 1874). In this book, Marey reported on his use of an ingenious array of graphic recording devices to dissect and analyze the components of human and animal movement. Also in 1874, Janssen made his sequence photographs of the solar eclipse; absorbing these developments in physiology and photography, Stanford was ready in 1877 to make another attempt to scientifically analyze the gait of his racing horses. He reengaged Muybridge, who had been busy publishing his South American photographs and had begun a vast panoramic study of the skyline of San Francisco, to make new photographs at Palo Alto. This time Muybridge was to record the complete gaits of the horses with the intent of producing an overall theory of their movements that would improve Stanford's training methods for competitive racing. In July, Muybridge succeeded in again taking individual instantaneous photographs of Occident trotting at speed that revealed "awkwardnesses" in the horse's gait as it had been habitually imagined by trainers and artists; proof of the realism of these photographs would come only in the next year, when Muybridge began to take serial chronophotographs.

With Stanford's financial support, Muybrige ordered twelve excellent Scoville wet-plate cameras from New York City, and equipped them with first-class Dallmeyer fast lenses. A special track was built with the cameras lined up on one side facing an eight-foot-high, thirty-foot-long white canvas marked off in twenty-one-inch segments. The bottom of the backdrop was ruled horizontally four, eight, and twelve inches above the track. Muybridge's fast-acting shutters, made by John D. Isaacs and Arthur Brown at Stanford's Central Pacific Railroad shops, were spring-driven drop shutters released electrically and mounted in front of the camera lenses. For a trotting horse with its sulky, the elecrical contact was closed by the metal wheel of the sulky contacting galvanized wires extending from the base of the backdrop and carried across the track itself, and for a horse and jockey threads releasing an electrical contact were stretched a few inches above the track and broken by the horse's feet as it passed. Beginning with photographs of the horse Abe Edgington trotting (with sulky), and then Sallie Gardner at the gallop (with rider only), taken before an invited group of sportsmen and newspaper

FIGURE 9. Leland Stanford's horse Sallie Gardner, photographed at the gallop by Eadweard Muybridge in 1878.

reporters, Muybridge now began an intensive two-year process of photographing Stanford's horses. He increased his setup to twenty, and then twenty-four cameras, and in the summer of 1879 added series photographs of the cow, deer, goat, ox, dog, and other animals to his repertoire, for which he devised a clockwork mechanism to set off the cameras, making his first sequences of human locomotion in August (Haas 1976, 112).

Following excited local newspaper reports by witnesses to the June 1878 photographic session (Haas 1976, 110), Muybridge quickly began to promote his work in public. He applied for patents on the shutter and the setup of his camera battery in late June and July (Muybridge 1878, 1878a), and lectured at the Art Association of California in San Francisco and other locations across the state, using lantern slides of his series photographs and comparing their record of movement to the traditional artistic representations of motion. Notices of Muybridge's work appeared in both professional photographic journals and the popular press; by the end of the year, news of the extraordinary photographs had spread to Europe, and Muybridge began exchanging correspondence with both Marey in Paris and the painter Thomas Eakins in Philadelphia. Both of his correspondents had used a Zoetrope to reconstitute the motion caught by Muybridge's serial photographs (in 1879 W. B. Tegetmeier copyrighted and sold in England a Zoetrope band using Muybridge's photographs); and Muybridge himself now turned to creating an instrument that he could use for the same purpose of reproducing his surprising photographs in his magic lantern lectures.

Based on the Phenakistiscope and described in the London Illustrated News as "a magic lantern run mad," Muybridge's projection device, the Zoöpraxiscope, in its first model combined an English biunial lantern with sixteen-inch-diameter rotating picture disks. A slotted metal shutter rotated in the opposite direction to the picture disk, and at the same speed. This instrument was not used, in fact, to project Muybridge's photographs: his disks contained only drawn images based on his photographs, and the drawings were slightly elongated to compensate for the foreshortening of the projected image caused by the timing of the two counterrotating disks.

All the same, given Muybridge's evident sprightliness as a lecturer, and his eagerness to entertain as well as inform his audience, the Zoöpraxiscope made a striking impression on audiences in the early 1880s. With his new device, and with his fame in photographic and artistic circles already established, Muybridge left for a lecture tour of Europe in late 1881. In Paris, he met the renowned physiological researcher Étienne-Jules Marey, who had been excited by the American's photographs three years earlier. Marey gave a party for Muybridge at his home, and their meeting was significant for both men. Marey introduced Muybridge to the new, faster, bromide gelatine dry plates that were just appearing on the market in Europe, and Muybridge gave Marey further insight into the uses of photography for the analysis of motion.

By the date of this meeting in 1881, Étienne-Jules Marey was fully established as a leading medical researcher. Born in the famous Burgundy wine-producing town of Beaune, France, on March 5, 1830, Marey enrolled at the faculty of medicine of the University of Paris in 1849 and qualified as a doctor in 1859 (the outstanding biography is Braun 1992). Four years later he began to devise his "methode graphique," which used a variety of ingenious mechanical devices to record physiological movement of and in the human body. He established a small independent laboratory in Paris in 1864, and published a work on the circulation of the blood, illustrated with graphs from his sphygmograph, an instrument for recording the human pulse (Marey 1863). Ever inventive and single-minded in his pursuit of his research projects, Marey continued to devise instruments that recorded physiological movements: thermographs to measure heat changes in the body (1864), pneumographs to study respiration (1865), myographs to record the function of voluntary muscles (1864–66), odographs to measure the steps taken during human and animal locomotion (1867–72), and many other ingenious devices. To interpret his graphic inscriptions of movement, Marey not only gave a close mathematical analysis to his results, but also arranged for Mathias Duval, a professor of anatomy at the École des beaux arts to make drawings based on his graphic records for use in the Phenakistoscope or Zoetrope. "This instrument, usually constructed for the amusement of children," wrote Marey in his classic work *La Machine animale*, "generally represents grotesque or fantastic figures moving in a ridiculous manner. But it has occurred to us that, by depicting on the apparatus figures constructed with care, and representing faithfully the successive attitudes of the body during walking, running, etc., we might reproduce the appearance of the different kinds of progression employed by man" (Marey 1874, 137). When Muybridge's serial photographs were published in France in December 1878, they confirmed Marey's own conclusion that all four feet of a horse were above the ground at one point during the gallop, and Marey began a brief correspondence with the California inventor, conducted in part in public through the pages of the journal *La Nature*.

Marey had dabbled in photography in the 1870s, attempting to record electrical charges in the muscular system, but found the medium inadequate to his purposes (Braun 1992, 46–47). In 1881 he returned to photographic experiments, constructing a "photographic gun" in the shape of a rifle, modelled on Janssen's apparatus, that was capable of taking twelve exposures on a single rotating plate in one second. A devoted aeronaut, Marey used this camera to study the flight of birds and bats. With the opening of his publicly funded Station physiologique in the Bois de Boulogne in 1882 he next began to construct a series of cameras using a single glass plate that recorded successive images of movement. His subject was frequently his new assistant at the laboratory, Georges Demenÿ, outfitted in an all-black costume with white tape sewn down the limbs of the body to highlight the essence of the body's movement during running, jumping, walking, and other exercises. These single-plate geometrical images, taken at various speeds up to $\frac{1}{1000}$ of a second by 1885, later inspired modernist painters like František Kupka, Marcel Duchamp, Anton Giulio Bragaglia, and others.

With his single-plate cameras, Marey could record consecutive images of a moving subject, and could vary the overlapping of the images by changing the speed of rotation of his single-slot rotating disk shutter. Varying the size of the opening in the shutter controlled the length of the exposure; adding additional slots to the disk allowed an even wider range of exposure times as well as controlling the overlap, or continuity, of the images, depending on the speed of the moving subject. Marey's photographs were taken against the solid background of an open-fronted shed constructed at the Station physiologique, which faced the sun to provide adequate illumination for the

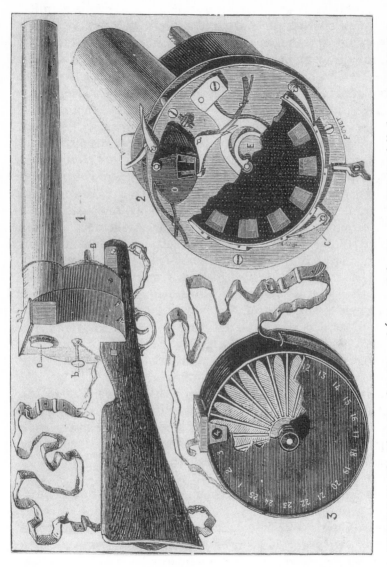

FIGURE 10. The Photographic Gun of Étienne-Jules Marey, 1882. Modelled on Janssen's Astronomical Revolver, Marey's apparatus took twelve images in one second, and was used for the photographic analysis of the flight of birds.

photographic experiments. For each of his various shutters, Marey could work out mathematically the precise relative time between each image, and then deduce the physiological data he needed on human and animal movement or the flight of gulls. As his research became more and more detailed, single-plate chronophotography began to show its limitations for his work in describing movement, and in 1888 Marey made a radical improvement in his recording methods, substituting a long strip of photographic paper for his glass plate, which produced separate images in sequences that were fully measurable, often aided by the inclusion of a chronometer in one corner of the frame that was photographed simultaneously and provided a time scale for the exact analysis of the row of individual pictures.

By this time Marey would have been aware of the massive project begun by Muybridge in August 1884 at the University of Pennsylvania after a long period of fundraising: the creation of a visual encyclopedia of human and animal movement. During 1884 and 1885, Muybridge took over 100,000 sequence photographs, of which 19,347 were published in the 781 plates of *Animal Locomotion: An Electro-photographic Investigation of Consecutive Phases of Animal Movements* in 1887. Although he had experimented with a Marey circular-shutter camera and a multiple-lens camera as well, this work in Pennsylvania was conducted with three new batteries of twelve cameras each using electrically released drop shutters. The pictures were taken in front of a black background marked with both vertical and horizontal lines, with one camera battery parallel to the background grid and the two others at either end, providing foreshortened views. Larger animals like horses and camels were photographed in the open air at the Zoological Gardens or the Gentlemen's Driving Park near Philadelphia.

The project was impressive in size and unique in scope, photographing both male and female models, often nude, sometimes in pairs, in a wide array of activities including walking, running, jumping, throwing, crawling, disrobing, turning, pouring water, wrestling, hammering, riding, going up or down stairs, meeting and passing. Its publication was taken as a scientific monument of photography and exerted considerable influence, with original subscribers to the massive volumes including the artists James Macneil Whistler, Léon Bonnat,

Lawrence Alma-Tadema, Holman Hunt, John Everett Millais, and many others. Excerpts of his obsessive work, first published as *Animals in Motion* and *The Human Body in Motion* at the turn of the century, are still in print today.

Yet as Marta Braun has scrupulously pointed out, some 40 percent of the plates in the work are not at all what Muybridge claimed them to be. They are assembled from different photographic sessions, excerpted from a single session and renumbered to give the impression of a continuous series, have missing or duplicated images within a series, or are reconstructed and reassembled in other ways (Braun 1992, 237–54). There is no concurrently photographed metronome or chronometer within the images, and the studies are freqently repetitive rather than explorative. The whole project does not proceed according to any overall scientific plan, notwithstanding its gridded background and the "regularity" of the presentations of the plates: it is more a monument to Muybridge's personal obsessions than to any rigorous scientific purpose.

Tireless, energetic, and hard-working, Muybridge was the great popularizer of chronophotography. After the publication of *Animal Locomotion* he took a concession at the Chicago World's Fair of 1893 and lectured daily on his work, projecting his images with a second model of the Zoöpraxiscope, now using an American-made science lantern modelled on those made by Duboscq in Paris, and twelve-inch-diameter picture disks. This second set of Zoöpraxiscope disks still used elongated and hand painted images, often highly colored. The drawn movements of animals and birds were often based on Muybridge's serial photographs, but some seem to be taken from printed Phenakistiscope disks, for example a monkey climbing vertically up a vividly colored and highly stylized palm tree.

Of over sixty picture disks in both sizes preserved at the Kingston Museum and Heritage Centre in Muybridge's hometown of Kingston-upon-Thames, England, only one disk uses photographic images. It is a sixteen-inch disk made by printing posed black-and-white photographs of the skeleton of a horse on glass plates, cutting the photographs into wedge-shaped pieces, and fixing the individual pieces to a circular glass backing. This disk, which did not use Muybridge's chronophotographs, is heavily retouched, with the images elongated and the positions of the skeleton's legs and hooves repainted.

After a disappointing reception at the World's Columbian Exposition in Chicago, Muybridge returned to England, where he continued to lecture and promote chronophotography through 1896. His work had a major influence on later experimenters in both Europe and America, but the odd combination of his aspirations and fixations makes his work a puzzling jumble of insights and banalities. Over a period of two decades, he only marginally improved his photographic apparatus, never changed his basic methods, and did not, in the end, contribute to any of the advances in photographic method that were pouring forth from his latter-day contemporaries. His celebrity and his very public life, along with the excitement his work created among photographers, inventors, and impresarios helped establish serial photography as the most modern phenomenon of the age. Yet his work was impulsive rather than rigorous, and it existed in a self-created world triangulated by science, celebrity, and entertainment, while really belonging whole-heartedly to none of those fields. A practical worker and tinkerer in the grand American tradition, it was perhaps Marey's status in Paris and a certain envy of the French doctor's well-equipped laboratory that turned Muybridge towards a scientism for which he was neither trained nor adapted.

In contrast, Marey's work through the same period remained a model of scientific rectitude and innovation as the French doctor constructed his first chronophotographic apparatus with a moving band of film. Reporting on his most recent work to the Académie des sciences on October 29, 1888, Marey exhibited photographs of the flight of a pigeon and the opening and closing of a hand taken at the rate of twenty images per second on Eastman paper roll film, with a camera using a circular disk shutter behind the lens. The paper stripping film was driven at a continuous speed past the camera's aperture, and stopped momentarily by an electomagnetic clamp synchronized with a slot in the disk shutter. A light leaf spring gently tensioned the film so that it did not tear while stopped to record the image. This camera with its series images was an improvement on Marey's single-plate methods, allowing him to analyze and measure the complete outline of a movement and the changes that occurred across the entire body. But the camera's electromagnet worked erratically with his unperforated film, and the images were irregularly spaced on the paper film, sometimes wide apart and sometimes overlapping.

Two years later Marey designed a new apparatus using transparent celluloid negative film in 1.10 meter lengths obtained from the firm of Georges Balagny. His new camera used a six-pointed star wheel to mechanically press a cylindrical clamp against the unperforated film and stop it momentarily for exposure. This camera had a shutter consisting of two circular disks, one rotating five times faster than the other; by altering the arrangement of the star wheel and the number of openings in one of the shutter disks, exposure rates of up to 100 images in a second could be obtained. In 1891 Marey constructed yet another camera that was able to use either glass plates or celluloid film, which allowed him a choice of methods depending on the specific movement he wished to record.

With all of this apparatus, Marey was intent on dissecting the principles of movement in birds, insects, animals, and humans. To confirm his analysis, he regularly cut up his original images and mounted them in an electric Zoetrope, in which he could see the reconstituted motion. He also possessed a special Zoetrope made by Ottomar Anschütz, now conserved at the Cinémathèque française (Mannoni 1996, 270, no. 842), which had three sets of viewing slots and which would allow the observed motion in the instrument to appear to be going forward or in reverse. Frequently, Marey also reordered or rephotographed his images so that the movement was not reproduced as the eye would observe it directly, but on an expanded time scale—in slow-motion, as it were—so that he could see in detail the precise mechanisms and pattern of motions otherwise too quick to be directly observed. Marey wrote the Académie des sciences on May 2, 1892, that he was constructing a projector for his serial images and intended to demonstrate it, but the demonstration never took place, perhaps because the irregularity of the images produced by all of his photographic apparatus precluded their direct use in such a device. But it is equally the case, as Marta Braun has written, that "Marey's lifelong desire to make visible what the unaided senses could not perceive would effectively bar him from avenues of research whose end was duplicating sensory perception, no matter how aesthetically pleasing the result" (Braun 1992, 174). Marey's purposes were always scientific, analytical, and revelatory; the work of reproducing photographed motion whether as instruction or entertainment was left to others, foremost among them the chronophotographer Ottomar Anschütz.

Born in Lissa, East Prussia (now Posen, Poland), on May 16, 1846, Ottomar Anschütz learned photography as a youth from his father, a well-known decorative painter in the region who opened a local studio for wet-plate photography toward the end of his life (the most thorough study is Rossell 1997). His further photographic studies were hardly provincial, as he worked briefly with the leading practitioners Ferdinand Beyrich in Berlin, then with Franz Hanfstaengl in Munich, and finally with Ludwig Angerer in Vienna before returning to Lissa and taking over his father's business in 1868 at the age of twenty-two. Anschütz travelled from town to town with a thirty-foot mobile studio, and began to pursue an interest in capturing natural movement with quick exposures: earlier in Vienna he had already received plaudits for an unusual photograph capturing the King of Saxony on horseback. By 1881 he was able to photograph marching soldiers, and the next year he photographed military maneuvers, including a sharp image of Crown Prince Friedrich passing in a wagon at a trot. In order to achieve even quicker exposures, he experimented with a focal-plane shutter and in 1884 began to take a remarkable series of pictures of storks in flight and at their rooftop nests. These dramatic images astonished the photographic world and brought Anschütz into the front rank of the photographers of the day. They also directly influenced the aviation pioneer Otto Lilienthal in his designs for gliders, much as Marey's dissection of the flight of birds had shaped the work of aeronaut Alphonse Péynaud a decade earlier.

By the end of the year Anschütz began to make systematic chronophotographs in the style of Muybridge, exhibiting a series of pictures of a galloping horse and a walking man taken with a battery of twelve cameras equipped with his further improved cloth focal-plane shutter. His work caught the attention of the authorities, and with a grant from the Culture Ministry of Prussia, Anschütz was able to build a new apparatus taking 24 separate photographs in about $^3/_4$ of a second. Constructed with his regular collaborator in Lissa, a neighboring organ-builder named

Schneider, this new apparatus had electrically released shutters controlled by a metronome in the circuit so that exposures were made at precisely determined intervals. Alternatively, the shutters were sometimes released by the forward movement of the subject breaking light threads, after the manner of Muybridge. To reduce the parallax inherent in a multiple-camera apparatus when it was located close to the subject and recording in-place movements, the nine-foot-long camera was mounted on a track and quickly moved past a single optical axis as the exposures were taken.

With this new apparatus and an assignment from the Prussian War Ministry, Anschütz travelled to Hanover in the summer of 1886, where he made over 100 series photographs, sometimes 15 sets of 24 pictures per day, at the Military Riding Institute. Intended to be used in improving riding instruction at the academy, these most famous of Anschütz's series photographs were acclaimed by the photographic community wherever they were exhibited. Although he had made no radical leap forward in chronophotography, the outstanding quality of Anschütz images were considered far superior to the work of both of his distinguished predecessors, particularly with regard to their fineness of detail, modelling of halftones, and clear rendition of motion in natural settings. "Chronophotographic series taken until now," wrote one observer in 1887, "have achieved more of an outline than a precisely modelled representation, as Muybridge with dark images against a bright background, and Marey with bright images against a dark background . . . just as in his individual high-speed photographs, Anschütz has reached the highest level in this area as well" (Schmidt 1887, 763).

The funding from the Cultural Ministry also gave Anschütz the opportunity to build special apparatus to reproduce the movements captured with his chronophotographic camera, and at one point he considered assembling a huge Muybridge-style atlas of gymnastic movements (Schmidt 1887, 763). He built several improved Zoetropes, one almost six feet in diameter and holding ninety-four images 10 cm square, and patented another in which the cylinder of the Zoetrope was formed by the band of images itself, with viewing slots incised in the band between the photographs (Anschutz 1890). He called his zoetropes "Schnellseher," or "quick-viewer," but his invented name is primarily identified with the eight or nine different mechanical devices he developed for viewing his chronophotographs, the prototype of which was finished in autumn, 1886, again constructed with the help of Schneider. All of the Anschütz machines worked on the same principle: positive transparencies were mounted around the outside of a disk, and as each image reached the viewing aperture of the apparatus, an electrical circuit was closed that set off a bright spark from a Geissler tube behind the glass plate. A sheet of milk-glass diffused the illumination across the viewing area, and the electrical spark was created by a charge from a Rühmkorff induction coil with two circuits: a primary low-voltage circuit linked to the turning disk, and a secondary high-voltage circuit connected to the Geissler tube. The synchronization was exact, and the results impressive.

The second model of the Schnellseher (often called the Tachyscope or Electrical Tachyscope in America) had a picture disk about five feet in diameter mounted on a freestanding rigid iron base and holding 24 four-inch glass transparencies. When it was seen in public for the first time, on March 19, 20, and 21, 1887, at the Culture Ministry in Berlin, it created a sensation. Crown Prince Friedrich Wilhelm, later the short-lived Kaiser Friedrich III, commented that the Schnellseher's truth to nature, down to the minutest details, was simply astonishing and that the very first glimpse almost took one's breath away (Schwartz 1892, 4). Anschütz began a series of demonstrations of his remarkable new device, and news of the Schnellseher quickly spread around the world: the *Philadelphia Photographer* wrote about the Anschütz "stroboscopic disk" in June 1887 (Hendricks 1961, 85), the photographic association in Frankfurt demanded a repeat performance of the machine when it was demonstrated in October, and it directly changed the course of Thomas Edison's experiments on the Kinetoscope (see chapter 5). But Anschütz had even greater plans for his device; he envisioned it not as a laboratory instrument for professionals or a novelty for photographers, but as a mass-produced apparatus for public instruction and entertainment. In January 1890 he demonstrated his "speaking portraits" to the Photographic Association in Berlin. Like Georges Demenÿ a year later in

Paris, Anschütz did not use a phonograph or other sound apparatus; his "speaking portraits" were simply "a new kind of series" that the report of this demonstration concluded was an achievement where "photography has reached one of the greatest triumphs that instantaneous work can celebrate, and it seems unquestionable that the time will come when such speaking portraits are prepared to order and are projected in the salons of the upper class by means of a specially adapted Schnellseher" (Anschütz 1890a, 69). Now Anschütz began to make arrangments for his apparatus to be manufactured for widespread sale and distribution.

The third model of the Schnellseher, still using the same fundamental structure of a circular image-disk illuminated by the intermittent spark of a Geissler tube, went into develop-

FIGURE 11. The second model of the Schnellseher, sometimes called the Elecrical Tachyscope, of Ottomar Anschütz, as illustrated by *Scientific American* in 1889.

ment at the renowned electrical manufacturing firm of Siemens & Halske in Berlin in 1890. In an unusual and pioneering artist/business partnership, the Charlottenburg Werke of Siemens & Halske would develop the new model Schnellseher together with Anschütz, who would control the exploitation of the device and, legally, order the machines from Siemens & Halske, who in turn would then be paid for their work for Anschütz by his customers. Displayed to widespread acclaim throughout the summer of 1891 at the Siemens & Halske stand of the International Electrotechnical Exhibition in Frankfurt-am-Main, the new cabinet-model Schnellseher was a coin-operated automat in a free-standing wooden cabinet, with a picture disk about four feet in diameter holding celluloid photographs 9 cm by 12 cm around its rim. In September 1891, Anschütz assigned North American rights to the machine to Arthur Schwartz & Co. in New York City, a small firm of photographic importers and suppliers, who quickly installed the "Electrical Wonder" at Koster & Bial's Music Hall and exhibited five machines at the Eden Musee in New York, with others sent to Boston and other cities. A year later, in November 1892, the world rights to exploit the machine went to the newly established Electrical Wonder Company of London, in which Anschütz himself was a stockholder.

The Anschütz Electrical Schnellseher (as this model was normally called) was perhaps the most remarkable piece of early cinema, or precinema, engineering design. Not only did it exhibit sharp and fully modelled images of a quality not to be seen in moving pictures for another decade or more, it also was capable of using picture disks with anywhere from 18 to 24 images, an immensely complex task of mechanical gearing and electrical timing. For a nickel in America, a penny in England, or ten pfennig in Germany, the machine ran for about twelve seconds, exhibiting two women dancing, soldiers marching, a pair of boxers in action, gymnasts tumbling, or the Anschütz signature images of a horse and rider taking a hurdle, among many other views. Nearly 34,000 people paid to see the Schnellseher at the Exhibition Park in Berlin in 1892, and it was also installed at the Chicago World's Fair in 1893, exhibited on The Strand in London, and ran at the Crystal Palace in south London. But if the machine was successful, the business arrangements Anschütz had made for its exploitation were considerably less so.

By early spring 1893, Arthur Schwartz & Co. in New York had given up their rights in the Electrical Schnellseher to the Electrical Wonder Company of London, whose general manager was none other than Arthur Schwartz again. In transferring the North American rights to the London company, a large order for new machines was left behind at Siemens & Halske; another large order had already been placed by the London company, for which the fledgling enterprise was soon unable to pay. By summer 1893, Siemens & Halske was left with fifty-two completed Schnellsehers for which Ottomar Anschütz, legally under their unusual agreement, owed the company more than 40,000 marks. Although over the next year and a half Siemens & Halske, heavy-industry manufacturers of railroad signals, electrical generators, and a wide variety of electrical goods, attempted to learn the entertainment business and to exhibit the Schnellseher on their own behalf "to give Herr Anschütz the opportunity to have the best possibilities of paying his bill with us" (Siemens 1893), the death of the Electrical Wonder Company of London was the end of the Electrical Schnellseher, and the end of the career of Ottomar Anschütz as a pioneer of moving pictures—with one astonishing exception.

Anschütz made one final, remarkable moving picture machine, the Projecting Electrotachyscope (Anschütz 1894). Using two large freestanding picture disks holding twelve images each and moving intermittently by means of a twelve-sided Maltese Cross mechanism, Anschütz projected forty different moving pictures on a huge screen measuring 19½ by 26¼ feet at the Post Office Building in Berlin on November 25, 29, and 30, 1894. In late February 1895, the apparatus was installed at the old Reichstag Building in Berlin, where it projected the Anschütz chronophotographs from February 22 through March 30 in a 300–seat hall; the box-office income for the month of March was 5,400 marks at an admission price of 1 and 1.50 marks. Siemens & Halske had again helped Anschütz with this machine, providing the powerful forty-ampere arc lamps used for illumination, manufacturing structural parts, and giving engineering advice through Anton Verständig. The Anschütz projector was then used in Hamburg from late May through mid-June 1895 by Dr.

Emil Kindler, who accompanied the moving pictures with a popular lecture on natural science. The whole arrangement was undoubtedly another attempt to reduce Anschütz's outstanding bill with Siemens & Halske. When they withdrew further support, no further known use was made of this unique apparatus, but it left an indelible impression on the press and the public. In late 1895 and througout 1896, as celluloid movies were shown in Berlin, first by the Skladanowsky brothers and then by Lumière's agents the Stollwerck Company and by others, many articles compared these new marvels to the Anschütz screenings. At the April 1896 opening of the first theater in Berlin at 21 Unter den Linden, the Kinematograph was called "fundamentally an improvement and perfection of the Anschütz Schnellseher," and the press notice of the first Bremen screenings of the Lumière Cinématographe also recalled the great chronophotographer's work (Rossell 1997, 5).

Chronophotography was an expensive medium, requiring unique cameras, costly lenses, specially built arrays of shutters and timing mechanisms, and sometimes precious celluloid film. Each of the three major experimenters had substantial financial support: Muybridge from the wealthy businessman Leland Stanford, Marey from the City of Paris, and Anschütz from the Culture Ministry of Prussia. Yet the medium seemed so useful, and promised such remarkable insights for science, that many others nonetheless took up chronophotography for their own purposes. In Scotland, the photographer John Annan published his own chronophotographs of a galloping horse in a riding manual in 1883 (Anderson 1883); in Boston, Dr. William Gilman Thompson took chronophotographs of the movements of the heart on apparatus "of his own devising" in 1886 (Anonymous 1886); in Prague, the physicist Ernst Mach used chronophotographs to study the flight of projectiles beginning in 1884 (David 1897, 199–209); and in Philadelphia, the painter Thomas Eakins used a Marey-style single-plate camera to study human movements in 1884 and 1885 (Frizot 1984, 135–37). The medical researcher Albert Londe built two multilens cameras in his laboratory at La Saltpêtière hospital in Paris with which he could study the movements of patients during epileptic fits, and investigate the movement of muscles during a variety of exercises. Active in chronophotography from 1882 through the turn of the century, Londe also later collaborated with General Sébert to develop special apparatus for the photography of cannon shells as an aid to the study of military ballistics (Bernard and Gunthert 1993).

A serious attempt to reduce the expense of chronophotography, and introduce it as a teaching medium in schools, was made by the Hanover physics teacher and gymnastics instructor Ernst Kohlrausch. His first device of 1890 arrayed twenty-four cameras and lenses in a ring that, when turned by a handle, passed an aperture with a spring-loaded shutter (Kohlrausch 1890). This was the first chronophotographic apparatus with multiple plates that made exposures from a single optical axis, eliminating the parallax inherent in the pictures of Muybridge and Anschütz. Searching for an affordable device, Kohlrausch made the ring of wood, its cover from cardboard, and the simple camera bodies from a combination of both. By 1892 he had developed a second camera, using again primarily his own funds, topped up by a small grant from the Prussian Culture Ministry. Still principally a ring design, this second camera used only four lenses (instead of twenty-four) fixed on a rotating disk in front of a light-tight camera "body," with a large plate-holding ring behind it. An arrangement of gears linked the two rotating wheels so that exposures and plates operated synchronously (Rossell 1995a, 28–29). For each of these cameras Kohlrausch designed and built a separate projecting apparatus; all four machines are preserved at the Deutsches Museum in Munich.

A teacher of physics and mathematics at Kaiser Wilhelms Gymnasium in Hanover, where he was also the gymnastics teacher, Kohlrausch devoted all of his spare time to the investigation of the mechanics of body movements in gymnastic exercise, on which he wrote a classic text (Kohlrausch 1881) and more than seventy articles. He served as well as an executive of numerous gymnastics organizations at the local, regional, and national level, and turned to chronophotography as a result of the work of Muybridge, Marey, and Anschütz, since he saw clearly that it could reveal the quick movements in gymnastic exercise that could not be perceived by the eye directly. He intended to use his apparatus in teaching, and to make it affordable for his fellow physical education teachers. He had little interest in the professional photographic societies, in the international chronophotographic fraternity, or in enter-tainment and showmanship. Although his attempt to create inexpensive chronophotographic apparatus attracted momen-tary attention in Berlin, there is no evidence that it was mar-keted publicly, and his isolation curtailed his influence on his contemporaries. His work is nonetheless an example of the widespread interest in chronophotography at the end of the nineteenth century, and of the many experimenters working to try and capture motion at the time. In Kohlrausch's case, there is strong evidence that he was the first chronophotographer to project moving pictures in public, at a meeting of the North West German Gymnastics Teachers Association in winter 1893 (Rossell 1995a, 29–30), since his vision of chonophotography as a classroom teaching tool required photographed motion to be both analyzed and then reproduced in the most naturalistic way possible. It was a vision of chronophotography that Kohlrausch shared with another committed gymnast, a figure who clearly recognized both the educational and entertainment potential of the medium: Marey's first assistant at the Station physi-ologique, Georges Demenÿ.

Born in Douai on June 12, 1850, Georges Demenÿ received his diploma in 1868 and enrolled first in the university at Lille, then moving to Paris to study mathematics at the Sorbonne in 1874. He was a passionate gymnast who had new and radical ideas about physical education, and in 1880 founded a circle of "rational gymnastics" that lobbied against the old-fashioned methods used in the schools for physical exercise (the outstand-ing study is Mannoni 1997). By that date Demenÿ had already met Marey, hoping to work with him on experiments that would advance his strong ideas about gymnastics, and when the Station Physiologique opened in 1882 Demenÿ became the assistant and *preparateur* at the new facility. With his gift for mathematics and sure hand for drawing, Demenÿ undertook much of the analysis of the chronophotographs taken at the lab-oratory, frequently also serving as the subject for the camera.

While Marey was away on his extended winter stays at his villa in Naples, Demenÿ took charge of the Station physi-ologique, and by autumn 1891 he had begun to investigate the application of chronophotography to the analysis of speech. Demenÿ thought that a photographic record of lip movements during speech could be a tool to help teach the deaf how to speak, and by October 1891 he had obtained a chronophotographic series of himself speaking the phrase "Je vous aime," which was published in *Paris-Photographe*, made with the Marey film camera and using mirrors to intensify the lighting on his face. In order to use these photographs, and others with phrases like "Vive la France!," Demenÿ cut the individual images from the film band, reproduced them on glass, and mounted the glass positives around the edge of a disk about 42 cm in diameter holding thirty pictures about 3 cm by 4.5 cm and turned by a crank. A rapidy counterrotating disk shutter with a single opening was mounted in front of the picture-disk; in principle, this was an enlarged magic lantern Wheel of Life as invented by Thomas Ross in 1871. By using a shutter that revolved several times for each revolution of the picture disk, Demenÿ avoided the optical foreshortening that plagued Muybridge's failed attempts to use series chronophotographs in his Zoöpraxiscope, although the very small photographs Demenÿ used would not allow much enlargement in projection, and the device was better suited to direct viewing. Demenÿ's new device was demonstrated for the Académie des sciences on July 27, 1891, and patented under the name Phonoscope in March of the next year (Demenÿ 1892).

The Phonoscope was exhibited at the International Exposition of Photography at the Palais des Beaux-Arts in Paris from April 20, 1892, along with one of Marey's single-plate chronophotographic cameras, a Marey film camera, and examples of the photographic work of the Station physiologique. Demenÿ recalled later that this exhibition of the Phonoscope resulted in "an avalanche of propositions" from many different "Barnums" seeking to exploit his invention (Mannoni 1995, 22). Demenÿ set up his own company to promote the apparatus, the Société Général du Phonoscope, in partnership with the Stollwerck brothers in Germany and William Gibbs Clarke in Switzerland. The statutes of the company (reproduced in Loiperdinger and Cosandey 1992, 24–26) anticipated the use of the Phonoscope for making "animated portraits" and for the projection of movement, as well as its use in combination with the phonograph, as a coin-operated automat, and in scientific research. To Demenÿ and his backers, it was the amateur or home market that promised the greatest return for the machine, and Demenÿ wrote enthusiastically, "How happy people would be if they could, in an instant, see again the living characteristics of a departed person. In the future, the still photograph, fixed in its frame, will be replaced by the animated portrait which, with a turn of a wheel, will be given life. The facial expressions will be preserved as the voice is preserved in the phonograph. One needs only to add the latter to the Phonoscope to complete the illusion" (Coe 1992, 56).

The Phonoscope also needed a source of images: it was still dependent on Marey's chronophotographic cameras for its content. Demenÿ then patented a new camera using 60 mm wide film on October 10, 1893, in which the take-up spool of the camera was mounted eccentrically, so that it pulled one new stretch of film into place for exposure at the camera's aperture on each revolution (Demeny 1893). When patents for this camera were filed in Switzerland and Germany only two months later (Demenÿ 1893a, 1893b), the apparatus had already been improved with one of the most signifigant early cinema intermittent devices. Instead of an eccentrically rotating take-up spool, the film was driven constantly through the camera, but a short bar, or roller, mounted eccentrically on a rotating gear was interposed between the camera's aperture and the take-up spool. Pressing the film band once on each revolution, the roller advanced just enough film to the camera aperture for a new exposure to be taken with precision. This was the origin of the "beater" movement, sometimes called a "dog" movement, which was later used by Thomas Armat in America in the apparatus that would become the Edison Vitascope, by W. C. Hughes for his Moto-Photograph, by the Prestwich Manufacturing Company in England, and in many other early film projection machines.

Meanwhile, relations between Marey and Demenÿ at the Station physiologique had been deteriorating. Demenÿ's devotion to research on physical education had at times led Marey to criticize his assistant's organization of the research program at the laboratory during Marey's long winter absences, when Marey wished to see more progress on experiments aimed at the topics of medicine and flight. In January 1893 Demenÿ established a small laboratory for Phonoscope experiments in the rue

Chaptal in the Paris suburb of Levallois-Perret, and he travelled to Switzerland and Cologne to confer with his partners. In April 1893 he wrote to a Paris city counsellor complaining about Marey's "senile and incoherent direction" of the Station physi-

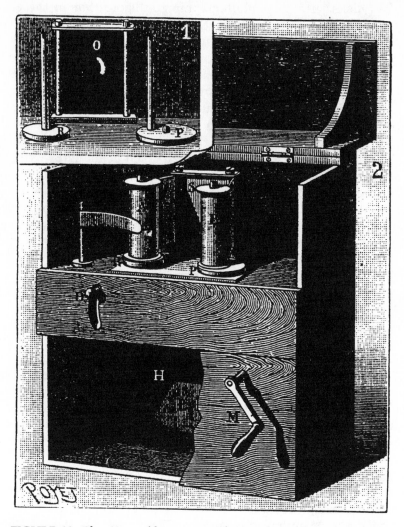

FIGURE 12. The 60mm film camera of Georges Demenÿ, first model, 1893. Used to provide images for the Phonoscope, the eccentrically mounted spool on the right provided the intermittent movement of the film band.

ologique (Mannoni 1994, 333). In July, a long negotiation between Lavanchy-Clarke and Marey came to nothing, as Marey apparently demanded 40 percent of any potential revenues from the Phonoscope. In October, Demenÿ wrote to the Lumière company in Lyon to see if they would coat the Phonoscope's glass disks with their photographic emulsions, but in the end the work was done by Jules Demaria in Paris (Manoni 1995, 26–27). Although Demenÿ continued to make adjustments to his camera, the Phonoscope company was making no commercial progress and Marey demanded that he give it up. When Demenÿ refused, he was dismissed from the Station Physiologique in March 1894, a break that became increasingly bitter over the next years, leading to many claims and counterclaims at first by Marey and Demenÿ themselves and later by their various supporters, with the result that much of the later writing about the contributions of the two men to the invention of moving pictures is intensely partisan.

With the departure of Demenÿ, work at the Station physiologique continued on animal locomotion with filmed subjects of horses, ducks diving into water, marching soldiers and the muscles used in bicycling, culminating in a large number of films of the athletes gathered for an international sports competition in Paris in 1900. Marey published his classic volume on *Le Mouvement* (Marey 1895), describing all of his scientific work and methods through 1894; he continued to write voluminously for scientific and medical journals through the turn of the century. Demenÿ, working from April 1894 at the Villa Chaptal, concentrated on his improved camera with its beater movement using film supplied by the European Blair Camera Company through its Paris representative George William de Bedts. He was full of plans of new apparatus, including a stereoscopic camera and projector, and a "large projector" intended for public exhibitions. Sketches of the mechanism for this second machine have been recently discovered, and they show a new intermittent movement using a pair of claws motivated by an eccentric cam: the kernel of the later Cinématographe Lumière. As Laurent Mannoni has carefully documented (Mannoni 1995, 32–38), these drawings were discussed at the Villa Chaptal in December 1894 when Louis Lumière made a visit to Demenÿ's workshop.

Demenÿ next concluded an agreement with de Bedts to retail his new Chronophotographe camera as well as the Phonoscope, the latter as an apparatus for making animated family portraits. At his laboratory, Demenÿ made 60 mm celluloid films of boxers, street scenes in the rue Chaptal, two women dancing the Can-Can, a train passing over a bridge in Paris, a baby's first steps, and about a hundred other subjects. Under increasing financial pressures, the inventor signed a contract with photographic manufacturer Léon Gaumont to make and sell both the Phonoscope and his Chronophotographe camera, which Gaumont renamed the Biographe as he placed both on the market in November 1895. Both failed: the rising tide of 35 mm celluloid film apparatus at the beginning of 1896 made the machines difficult to supply with new film subjects, while 35 mm apparatus could rely on a large existing stock of films from several sources. With his plans increasingly moribund, Demeny produced one more apparatus, a new 60 mm film camera and projector using perforated film that had some success when marketed in 1896. He ceded all interests in his patents to Gaumont, who adapted Demenÿ's designs to 35 mm film and successfully exploited the beater movement for several years, but the inventor had by then returned to his first love: research in physical education. He organized an international congress on physical training in Paris for the Exposition of 1900, and two years later was named Professor of Applied Physiology at Joinville, where he remained until his retirement.

The chronophotographers had the ability to reproduce completely natural motion on a screen in front of an audience, as Anschütz, Demenÿ, and probably Kohlrausch all demonstrated well before 1895. Since these inventors all used individual transparencies in their projection apparatus, the only thing their "movies" lacked was duration; later systems using long bands of celluloid film allowed the photographing and reproduction of movements that were not repetitive and periodic. But if their representation of movement was limited in time, the work of the chronophotographers retained distinct advantages over the celluloid moving picture systems available through at least the end of the century. Ernst Kohlrausch succinctly defined these advantages at a demonstration he gave of his own projection device at the Congress for Internal Medicine in Wiesbaden in 1898. Noting that the new cinematographic methods were better suited for movements of long duration, Kohlrausch nonetheless contended that in comparison to celluloid projection, "to my mind, 1) the images on the glass plates are much larger, clearer and richer in detail, and allow much bigger and clearer reproduction in projection; and 2) the images are presented with a completely equal rhythm, which for every scientific investigation of movement is recognized as a significant preference. In addition, the pictures, when they are properly fixed, appear completely steady on the screen and the chattering and jumping of the image which is so disturbing in the cinematograph is completely absent in my type of projection" (Kohlrausch 1898, 569). It would be the introduction of a new material into the photographic world that became the key to the invention of the cinema that grew into the next century's mass entertainment medium, a transparent, flexible base for holding photographic emulsions called celluloid.

CHAPTER FOUR

The Search for a Material:
The Development of Celluloid

The development of long flexible bands of celluloid film coated with photographic emulsion played a crucial role in the invention of motion pictures in their modern form. The inclusion of celluloid film bands in the peep-show Kinetoscope, 35 mm wide and with four perforations for each image frame on either side of the strip, a format still used today for theatrical movies, is perhaps the central contribution of Thomas Edison and W. K. L. Dickson to the invention of the cinema. Celluloid also holds a special place of honor as the first of the modern plastics, the first synthetic material used to replace scarce natural resources or through its workability to allow new forms and uses that have been central to daily life in the twentieth century.

Like the mechanical technology of the cinema, the chemistry of celluloid was also a newly emerging field in the late 1880s. The difficulties of forming celluloid into thin, flexible, transparent strips, of adhering a photosensitive emulsion to a celluloid support, and of producing a product that was consistent from batch to batch, without blistering, fogging, or light flares caused in the manufacturing process, were immense challenges not quickly solved. By 1896, there were only four major producers of photographic celluloid films in the world, each still experimenting to find the best chemical formula and manufacturing process for the new material: Victor Planchon in France, the Eastman Dry Plate Company and the Blair Camera Company in America, and the European Blair Camera Company in England. Their production problems were solved in parallel with the resolution of the mechanics of film projection, and only a few other small producers slowly joined these pioneering firms, as in the period up to 1900 the making of celluloid film largely remained, as today, in the hands of a limited number of companies.

The origins of celluloid lie in the discovery of two earlier organic compounds: nitrocellulose, popularly known as gun-cotton and used as an explosive substitute for gunpowder, and collodion, which became widely used as a carrier of photosensitive materials and greatly improved the speed of exposure of photographic plates. After early experiments by the pioneering French chemists Henri Braconnot in 1833, who combined nitric acid and potato starch into a material he called "xyloidine," and Théophile-Jules Pelouzé, who used nitric acid and paper to make "pyroxyline," the breakthrough to a useful organic compound came in 1846 from the discoverer of ozone, Christian Friedrich Schönbein, professor of chemistry at the University of Basel.

Schönbein wrote his colleague Michael Faraday in England on February 27, 1846, that "I have of late also made a little chemical discovery which enables me to change *very suddenly, very easily* and *very cheaply* common paper in such a way, as to render that substance exceedingly strong and entirely waterproof" (Kahlbaum 1899, 153). With his next letter to Faraday, on March 18, 1846, Schönbein included a sample "of a transparent substance which I have prepared out of common paper. This matter is capable of being shaped out into all sorts of things and forms and I have made from it a number of beautiful vessels" (Kahlbaum 1899, 155). Schönbein also sent samples of his new material to the eminent chemist J. C. Poggendorf in Germany, who suggested its use as a substitute for window glass, and as a tough and long-wearing replacement for paper in the making of bank notes.

Continuing his experiments into the reaction of acids on nitrated cotton, Schönbein on March 11, 1846, announced his discovery of gun-cotton, suggesting that he had found a major new explosive. While news of this substitute for gunpowder spread quickly across the industrialized world, Schönbein patented his discovery in England and America (Schönbein 1844a, 1846b) and continued to explore the products of specialized reactions between nitrated cellulose (pyroxylin) and various solvents. The key solvent that emerged was ethyl alcohol; it produced from moderately nitrated cellulose a viscous, colorless liquid that, when dried on a flat surface turned into a transparent sheet whose brittleness and strength could be varied according to the proportions of the ingredients in the original mixture. By January 1847 this new substance, called collodion in its liquid form, was proposed as a waterproof and flexible bandage for wounds and medical surgery by the Boston physician J. Parker Maynard. Beginning in 1851, liquid collodion found a significant and lasting use as a vehicle for photosensitive emulsions, first suggested by Gustav le Gray, patented by the Boston photographer James A. Cutting (Cutting 1854), and then developed as a practical medium of photography by Frederick Scott Archer in England in his wet-plate collodion process, or Archerotype (Archer 1855).

The use of collodion emulsions in photography was a giant leap forward from the existing daguerreotype and albumen processes since it allowed much shorter exposure times for a photographic subject; this substantial decrease in the length of a photographic exposure led directly to the instantaneous series photographs of Eadweard Muybridge, as well as to the development of more portable cameras like those made by Ottomar Anschütz, whose speed of exposure made sharp and vivid images of the natural world possible, and liberated photography from the confines of the professional portrait studio.

Solid celluloid was developed over many years of private experimentation by Alexander Parkes, the son of a brass lock manufacturer in Birmingham, England. Palkes exhibited his new material at the Crystal Palace exhibition of 1862, winning a bronze medal, and in 1865 he announced publicly his ability to make nitrocellulose into a stable, fully formable material by combining it with any of several plasticizer-solvents (Parkes 1865). This new material, which he called Parkesine, could be easily colored and had a smooth and unblemished surface. It also could imitate the properties of many other natural substances, depending on the precise type and amount of solvent used, and his initial disclosure of the new discovery, at the Society of the Arts in London on December 20, 1865, described Parkes's success in "producing a substance partaking in a large degree of the properties of ivory, tortoise-shell, horn, hard wood, india rubber, gutta percha, &c." (Friedel 1983, 8).

Parkes was a prolific inventor, who lived from the sale of his more than sixty patents in metallurgy, electroplating, and chemistry. He invented a process for desilverizing lead that was widely used long into the twentieth century, as well as methods for making seamless tubes and printing rollers. "More fortunate than many inventors," one biographer wrote, "this life of intellectual adventure never reduced him to penury" (Goldsmith 1922, 36). But Parkes was unsuccessful in launching his celluloid plastic as a marketable substance. He attempted to mass-produce the new material using the cheapest cotton remnants available, which contained many impurities, such as husks and pieces of wire. Due to these impurities and Parkes's imprecise understanding of the chemistry of making the new material, the quality of Parkesine varied widely from batch to batch, and the company that Parkes founded in 1866 to exploit his discovery was bankrupt by 1868, after failed attempts to make imitation ivory and pearl goods, including knife handles, earrings, piano keys, pens, buttons, combs, and all sorts of inexpensive consumer goods. Parkes also tried to develop industrial uses for his material, including its adaptation as an insulating material for electrical wires and telegraph poles, gear wheels, and various components of spinning machinery. Parkes returned to the metals industry after 1868, but the works manager of the short-lived Parkesine Company became obsessed with the new material and spent the next two decades attempting to make it into a practical manufacture. This was Daniel Spill, who had originally come to Parkes to negotiate a license for using Parkesine to improve the waterproof properties of the textiles produced at his brother's factory. Spill ultimately took out a patent on what would be the most important of all the nitrocellulose solvents, camphor (Spill 1869), but his ventures were also economically unsuccessful even though Spill persisted in trying to find the correct formula for a useful and stable collodion plastic. While neither pioneer was fully successful in bringing a practical celluloid into common use, Spill had a continuing involvement in the celluloid story: he initiated a long, complex, and arduous patent lawsuit against the eventual discoverer of a useful celluloid, in an action lasting from 1876 to 1884 that left him a ruined man and presaged the many suits and countersuits of the early days of the film inventors.

Commercial success in manufacturing the new material was finally achieved and patented by an American, John Wesley Hyatt of Albany, New York, in 1870 (Hyatt 1870); he named his formable plastic "celluloid." Trained as a printer, Hyatt used a mixture of pyroxyline and camphor, which was then molded under both heat and pressure to create a new material that was stable and hard in nearly any shape. Yet from the very beginning, when Hyatt and his brother Isaiah Smith Hyatt registered the Celluloid Manufacturing Company in Albany on January 28, 1871, the new material was inextricably linked to its explosive source, gun-cotton. When the Hyatt brothers tried to interest a manufacturer of hard rubber goods in their substitute material, their overtures were refused with the advice that their new process was so dangerous that they were more than likely to blow themselves up (Friedel 1983, 15). Recapitalizing the Celluloid Manufacturing Company, and moving to Newark, New Jersey, in late 1872, the Hyatt brothers improved the manufacturing apparatus necessary for the mass production of their new material. Now, they were fully in business, if only a practical and economic use for celluloid could be found.

Hyatt's original experiments were encouraged by a prize of $10,000 offered by the Phelan & Collender company in New York for patent rights in any suitable substitute for ivory in the manufacture of billiard balls, and his first celluloid-related patent was for a collodion coating for billiard balls made out of a composition of marble dust and glue (Hyatt 1869; Parkes had taken out a British patent for billiard balls made of Parkesine in 1868). But the Hyatt imitations were not durable, and his first successful manufacture was in substituting celluloid for the hard rubber used in dental plates. As they struggled to refine this product and create a market for their new material, the Hyatt brothers next took a conservative but crucial business decision. Rather than manufacture themselves the hundreds—perhaps thousands, no one yet knew—of items where celluloid could act as a substitute for more expensive or less appropriate natural materials, the Celluloid Manufacturing Company would supply bulk celluloid in sheets, rods, or blocks, and issue licenses to established manufacturers, who would pay a royalty for the use of the material. The Hyatt's style of operation was similar to the one later utilized by Thomas Alva Edison, when he decided not to exhibit and exploit his Kinetoscope viewer himself, but instead issued franchises for its exhibition through territorial agents.

By 1880 the Celluloid Manufacturing Company had issued licenses to almost two dozen firms, who engaged in the manufacture of celluloid dental plates, harness trimmings, knife and cutlery handles, emery wheels, brushes, shirt cuffs and collars, shoes, piano keys, and a variety of jewelry items and fancy goods. John Wesley Hyatt received sixty-one patents between 1869 and 1891 for various celluloid-related processes (Friedel 1983, 56–58), some of which were for the development of specific products like collars and combs; a few independent companies were also begun by the Hyatts to manufacture finished celluloid goods, again just as Thomas Edison was doing at the time with his various electrical companies.

Through the 1870s, celluloid products made their way into the marketplace as a replacement for ivory, horn, and tortoise-shell in combs, as an acceptable fashion item in the steadily increasing use of detachable collars and cuffs, and either as an imitation of natural materials or as an additional raw material that created new forms in fancy goods and novelties, including buttons, necklaces and brooches, watch chains, cribbage boards, key rings, dominoes, soap dishes, and a wide variety of other products. For the next twenty years, celluloid was identified with cheap goods and toys; in 1893 the French inventor Henri Lioret supplied Émile Jumeau with a small celluloid disk record to provide the voice for a talking doll, and a few years later used celluloid in his loud-speaking phonograph, intended for public performances where loud volume was required. The celluloid cylinder of his Lioretgraph apparatus allowed grooves of greater amplitude than those that could be impressed in wax, leading to the machine's greater amplification of the recorded sound (Chew 1981, 61–62). The exception to these passing fancies, and the major lasting use of celluloid, was in the field of photography.

Photographers were quick to look to the new material as a substitute for the heavy, breakable glass plates that were a basic component of their medium, but they were slow to adopt its use in any widespread way. The profession had long sought some kind of relief from both the weight and fragility of glass plates, and Alexander Parkes took out a provisional patent for substituting his flexible, unbreakable material for the glass used in photography as early as 1856. The full patent was never issued, as Parkes abandoned it, but his foresight was remarkable as he proposed "substituting for the sheets of glass a sheet of collodion of sufficient thickness to support the prepared film; a thick layer of collodion may be first formed on the glass, and on this layer the film of prepared collodion may be produced, and the picture taken thereon and suitably varnished or protected; afterwards the whole may be stripped from the glass together" (Parkes 1856, 1) Daniel Spill later suggested the same use of celluloid in photography at a lecture to the London Photographic Society in 1870, when he proposed that his xylonite could be "a flexible and structureless substitute for the glass negative supports" (Friedel 1983, 91). The French photographers David and Fortier explored using liquid celluloid to form sheets on a heated glass plate and then coating it with gelatin emulsion in the early 1880s (Harding 1995, 23), but it was not until November 1888 that celluloid became available as a base for photographic plates, when John Carbutt of the Keystone Dry Plate Company in Philadelphia announced that he was now making sensitized sheets of celluloid for the photographic trade. It was with Carbutt sheet film that W. K. L. Dickson began his experiments on the Kinetoscope in its early form as a cylinder machine at the Edison laboratory in West Orange in the summer of 1889.

An Englishman who had emigrated to America and became a major manufacturer of gelatine dry plates, Carbutt introduced several innovative photographic products in the late 1880s, including the first orthochomatic dry plates marketed in the United States, nonhalation plates, a special plate for lantern slides, and a variety of engraving plates. In marketing the transparent, lightweight, and unbreakable celluloid dry plates as a substitute for glass, Carbutt purchased the base celluloid sheets from the Hyatts, who made clear celluloid blocks that they could slice accurately to a thinness of up to ten one-thousandths of an inch on their patented machinery (Hyatt 1884). Carbutt's new plates were widely reported in the photographic press, and were also marketed, by mail "without fear of breakage" in England and the Continent beginning in late 1888. Within a year, the British firms of E. G. Wood and William England were offering their own celluloid plates.

Others suggested celluloid as a replacement for glass in lantern slides: the weight of several boxes of lantern slides for an evening's entertainment or instruction was a significant addition to the paraphernalia a travelling lanternist needed to carry, and the heavy glass slides inhibited as well the lanternist's desire for the faster and faster changing of slides during a program. Walter Poyner Adams proposed an ingenious celluloid film band for the magic lantern in 1888, where "Gelatine, Algin Compounds and Celluloid are suitable for this purpose" and the strip of pictures was mounted on rollers, where it was "wound on to one roller from another, so that each view passes the condenser in turn. The movement of the rollers may be accomplished by hand or mechanically" (Adams 1888). E. T. Potter made a similar suggestion the same year, when he proposed moving a continuous band of celluloid lantern slides by means of a clockwork mechanism (Potter 1888).

The creation of suitably thin transparent celluloid films whose flexibility would allow long bands of celluloid to be used in either taking or projecting photographs required a subtle change in the chemical composition of the material. The appropriate solvent for nitrated cellulose in this case was amyl acetate, patented by the chief chemist of the Celluloid Manufacturing Company, John H. Stevens, in 1882 (Stevens 1882) and the origins of a successful thin, flexible film of celluloid useful in photography lay in the experiments of two very different men: the photographic plate manufacturer George Eastman in Rochester, New York, and the part-time lanternist and full-time preacher the Rev. Hannibal Williston Goodwin in Newark, New Jersey.

A former bank clerk with a passion for photography and an unmatched business acumen, George Eastman was an important maker of quality gelatin-coated photographic dry plates and other photographic materials in the early 1880s. In late 1883 he began working with another Rochester, New York, camera designer, William H. Walker, to devise a viable roll-film system. Roll film would allow the taking of a number of photographs without the necessity of preparing and carrying a separate set of glass plates for photographic negatives, which would then need to be loaded in the camera one by one. A roll of film in the camera would also replace a number of ingenious but awkward devices using springs, plungers, gravity, or levers in portable cameras that permitted up to a dozen photographs to be taken before the photographer needed to return to the darkroom to reload the camera. The idea of a photographic system that would replace glass negatives was not new: a gutta-percha stripping system, where a collodion emulsion was dried onto a flexible surface and then stripped away for development of the image, was suggested by Frederick Scott Archer in his 1855 patent; the mounting of the emulsion on black calico cloth was tried by Captain H. J. Barr the same year; and Leon Warnerke marketed a roll system camera using collodion or gelatin emulsion on a paper backing in England in 1875 (Coe 1978, 79–81).

Eastman and Walker brought their roll film holder, which the *British Journal of Photography* (August 28, 1885) called "one of the most perfect pieces of mechanism yet introduced into photography," onto the market in 1885. Eastman's combination of a wooden roll holder, supplied with an oversize back that could be cut down to replace the glass-plate holders of many different cameras, plus a paper stripping film called American Film, where the developed emulsion was removed from a paper backing leaving a transparent negative for printing, was not only a rapid success, but was also imitated quickly by many other manufacturers in America and Europe, including Morgan and Kidd, the Blair Camera Company, and the photographic jobbers E. & H. T. Anthony. Eastman's next major step was to integrate his roll holder inside a simple box camera utilizing his stripping film, which after some experimentation produced the Kodak system, marketed in June 1888.

The Kodak revolutionized still photography, bringing picture-taking into the hands of a mass public, particularly through Eastman's strategy of preloading his new camera with a 100–image roll of paper negative stripping film that was then returned intact to the Eastman Dry Plate company for development. The camera was reloaded and returned to the customer with the developed nega-

tives and a postive print of each successful image. The camera cost
$25; the developing and printing service, plus a new roll of film,
$10. The inexpensive outfit was marketed at a time of widespread
interest in photography, when eager amateurs were exploring all of
the possibilities of the medium. Not only simple to operate, a photographer now no longer needed to learn the chemistry of developing and printing his or her own pictures, and was no longer
required to be involved in the mechanics and chemistry of photographic technology. The Kodak immensely increased the popularity of taking pictures and expanded the market for photographic
apparatus and film. But its success also left Eastman with a significant problem: the complexity of handling, developing, and printing his paper-backed stripping film.

The backing of Eastman's film was made from paper manufactured with mineral-free water at the Rives factory in France.
This chemically inert base was then coated with a layer of
gelatin that was soluble in water, on top of which was applied a
layer of photosensitive gelatin specially formulated to be less
water-soluble. Later, a nonreactive gelatin layer was also coated
on the back of the paper, to help reduce the tendency of the
paper to curl while dry in the camera. The exposed stripping
film was developed and fixed, and then floated emulsion-side
down in a bath of water. A glass plate in the water was raised to
the developed film, which was then squeegeed onto the glass; a
warm water bath then dissolved the inner gelatin layer and the
paper backing was removed. When dry, a wax coating on the
glass allowed the hardened gelatin negative to be stripped from
the glass so that prints could be made, or, alternatively, the negative was left on the glass, producing a glass-plate negative.

The many complexities in both the manufacture and the
subsequent developing process of his stripping film led Eastman,
even as he introduced his product to the market and developed
the Kodak camera, to continue to search for another material for
the film backing, preferably a transparent one where the negative layer would not have to be painstakingly and delicately
removed from its support to make positive prints. He tried solutions of pyroxylin, Irish moss, Japanese isinglass, and seaweed,
among many other substances (Jenkins 1975, 127), but had no
success. By March 1888, just before the introduction of the
Kodak, he began to consider the use of celluloid, and by the end

of the summer assigned his chief chemist, Harry M. Reichenbach, the task of trying to find an appropriate solvent that would dilute celluloid so that a thin film of regular consistency could be manufactured as the base of a photosensitive film.

Enough progress had been made by April 1889 that two patent applications for the new process were filed, one in Eastman's name for the machinery intended for the manufacture of thin celluloid film (Eastman 1889) and one in Reichenbach's name for the chemical composition of the celluloid mixture (Reichenbach 1889), since Eastman wanted to particularly recognize him for his contributions to their joint efforts. Production of the new celluloid-backed roll film began in August 1889, with the fluid celluloid flowed across twelve glass tables each 3½ feet wide and 50 feet long; the flowed celluloid was left to dry and harden overnight, and the resulting celluloid sheets were coated with photographic emulsion the next day. After again drying, the finished film was cut into various sized sheets for plate cameras and strips for roll holders.

Demand for the new product quickly overwhelmed Eastman's production capacity, and the company's head of sales, Gustav Milburn, told the *St. Louis and Canadian Photographer* in October 1889 that "orders for the films are so great that although they [the company] have a large plant for the express purpose of manufacturing them, still they cannot fill but comparatively a small percentage of their orders, making some skeptical people say that they believe the Eastman Company have been forced to discontinue manufacturing the films. The facts are that the Eastman company are working night and day on these films, and are producing from 600 to 800 lineal feet of transparent film, forty-one inches wide, per day; one-third of this product going to Europe" (389–90). Eastman's production facilities were moved to a new factory with twelve plate glass tables each 200 feet long in June 1891, a capacity that was again doubled the next year. To supply European customers, production of celluloid roll film began at the end of 1891 in a new Eastman factory at Wealdstone, just outside London, on twelve glass tables 80 feet long and 42 inches wide, which was capable of producing 960 linear feet of film a day (Harding 1996, 36).

In September 1889, the patent examiner declared that the Eastman and Reichenbach applications interfered with each other, and with a prior application filed in May 1887, by the Rev. Hannibal Goodwin of Newark, New Jersey. Goodwin was a prototypical American tinkerer. An Episcopalian and graduate of the General Theological Seminary in New York City, his service in various parishes in New Jersey and California included delivering illustrated lectures for young people. To create his own illustrated materials, he began to take an interest in photomechanical printing in the late 1870s, while rector of the House of Prayer in Newark, New Jersey, and received several patents on the production of halftone screens, also founding the Hagotype Company for their production. Acquiring a Sciopticon lantern for his illustrated presentations, he then began to make photographic slides, and turned his attention to a substitute for their heavy double-glass enclosures.

For nearly a decade Goodwin fiddled with various compounds of celluloid in an attic laboratory, and applied for a patent on May 2, 1887, that named celluloid as a replacement for glass plates in photography, and was very broadly written, as Goodwin staked his claim to a wide variety of substitutes for glass plates and paper, and for the processes of making them—particularly a process of flowing viscous celluloid over a flat glass or metal surface. It was this application that created an interference with those of Eastman and Reichenbach. Goodwin's actual patent was not issued until eleven years later in 1898 (Goodwin 1887), after many modifications and appeals within the patent office: litigation over the patent was not finally resolved until 1914, over a decade after Goodwin's death, with a victory for his heirs. Eastman's settlement to the Ansco Company, the owners of the deceased Goodwin's patent and of his small Goodwin Film & Camera Company, was $5 million for all past sales of Eastman Kodak film and for a licence to continue manufacture celluloid film for the year and a half remaining on the Goodwin patent. Other infringing manufacturers paid just over $300,000. (For the entire, epic story of this litigation, see Jenkins 1975, 125–30, 146–47, 156–58, 248–51, 332–35.)

Although Goodwin made little practical contribution to the manufacturing technology of celluloid film, he envisioned clear, flexible celluloid as a vehicle for photographic images, and described the making of celluloid film by flowing it in a liquid state over a flat surface. His influence extended throughout the

1890s, and after, as the many unresolved questions about his patent claims inhibited other American manufacturers from entering the new field of manufacture. Only one other American company brought celluloid roll film to the market: the Blair Camera Company of Boston. They avoided patent litigation from either Goodwin or Eastman by purchasing their base material from the Celluloid Manufacturing Company and then coating it with their own photographic emulsions at a factory in Boston.

Founded by Thomas Henry Blair, an immigrant from Nova Scotia who had started as a manufacturer of a portable wet-plate system for professional photographers, Blair attempted to build an organization that for a few years was the only serious rival to the Eastman company. Through his own inventions, as well as through acquiring other small manufacturers and contracting for patents that avoided Eastman's proprietary holdings, the string of companies associated with Blair offered a full range of photographic products, including amateur roll film cameras and plate cameras, photographic papers and chemicals, and celluloid roll films. Primarily a camera manufacturing company that branched out into a wide variety of photographic accessories, Blair marketed a roll film camera in 1888, the Hawk-Eye designed by Samuel N. Turner, and by summer 1890 bought up a Boston maker of celluloid sheet film and began to investigate the making of celluloid roll film for his Hawk-Eye camera.

Blair persuaded the Celluloid Manufacturing Company to produce a thinner sheet of material than had been their standard; they used a different manufacturing procedure than Eastman, flowing their celluloid continuously over a large copper drum. This method produced a somewhat thicker sheet, not flexible enough for the tight winding into rolls which Blair needed. Because the Celluloid Company also used a different chemical formula than Eastman that helped the celluloid to dry quickly and flow smoothly, and that included acetone and acetanilid (instead of Eastman's camphor), the resulting sheets had a slightly frosted texture. As Thomas Edison and W. K. L. Dickson worked out the final form of their Kinetoscope viewer, this made the Blair film particularly suited to their apparatus, since a viewer saw the films by transmitted light: the slightly translucent quality of Blair film helped spread the illumination across the frame of the film. (Throughout 1896, this translusence also caused many reports of "poor" film showings, when films on frosted celluloid intended for use in the peep-show Kinetoscope were used for projection, producing a weak image on the screen.) Virtually all Kinetoscope prints were made on Blair film stock through the end of 1896 (Musser 1990, 81).

Blair developed his own continuous drum method of coating celluloid, an extension of the Celluloid Company's manufacturing technology, but in April 1893 Blair was removed from the management of his company in a shake-up orchestrated by his financial investors. He left the United States for England, where he founded the European Blair Camera Company, taking with him permission to use several of his key patents in his new concern and his wide contacts among the East Coast photographic manufacturers. With offices in London and a factory at Foot's Cray, Kent, Blair recreated his American firm on European soil, offering a full line of roll film cameras, photographic supplies and accessories, and, importantly, celluloid film in sheets and rolls. In the production of celluloid roll film the Americans were two or more years ahead of any European manufacturer, and it was the European Blair Camera Company that supplied raw film stock for the first experiments of the Lumière Brothers in France, for Birt Acres and Robert Paul in England, for Oskar Messter in Germany, and for most of the other pioneer inventors and filmmakers in England and on the Continent.

Part of the Blair economic success with roll film was due to a series of production problems experienced by Eastman and his associates in the early 1890s. The chemistry of celluloid production was still a magical art, and the problems of making a consistent product were legion. The consistency of the fluid celluloid needed to be precise, just viscous enough that the material flowed evenly and smoothly to the required thickness and did not spill off the glass tables, yet dilute enough that it did not blister or crack or show any other imperfection. The photographic emulsion was exceedingly difficult to adhere thoroughly to the celluloid base, and was also prone to flares caused by static electricity during its removal from the tables, while the applied emulsion needed to be consistent in its photographic sensitivity.

All manufacturers struggled with this byzantine set of interrelated factors throughout the 1890s, and the designer/inventors of early cinema apparatus took the inconsistencies of thickness, of shrinkage in development, and of adhesion that were present in early film stock into account as they constructed their machines. It is not unusual to find a mechanical element included in a patent "so as to prevent the possibility of the film slipping by reason of variations in its thickness," or an explanation of the apparatus that claims the film "may be moved the proper distance for exposing the successive pictures without liability to slipping due to the varying thickness of the film" (both from Thomas Armat's second Vitascope patent of September: Armat 1896, 4, 5).

Eastman's production difficulties in 1892 and 1893 as personnel in the film-coating department changed (Jenkins 1975, 152–55) left Blair virtually the only supplier of celluloid roll film in a rapidly expanding market. As demand for roll celluloid increased with the invention of moving pictures, the Eastman Company had to claw their way back into the market. But with the shift to projected films through 1896, both the Blair Camera Company and European Blair had to change the basic formulation of their celluloid base, since a clear base, and not a translucent one, was now required for screen projection. In this change, they fell back into one of the basic problems that had plagued manufacture five years earlier: the photosensitive emulsion would not adhere properly to the celluloid base. It was the beginning of the end for their role as a pioneer supplier of celluloid film to the cinema trade. Combined with patent litigation reverses to Eastman on their roll camera systems and the loss of Thomas Henry Blair's inventive abilities, the Blair Camera Company in the United States was finally sold to Eastman in early 1899; European Blair continued in business until June 1903. Eastman thereby obtained Blair's patents in the United States on the drum machinery for continuous casting of celluloid film, which again increased his production capacity in a market that was now explosively expanding due to the demand of the growing cinematographic industry.

In the production of celluloid film, European manufacturers developed their own materials two to three years later than the Americans, and the impetus behind its production was undoubtedly the creation of film bands for motion pictures. When the Kinetoscope arrived in Europe in autumn 1894, it arrived with its forty-odd feet of 35 mm celluloid film. Although

there were European producers of sheet celluloid for photographic plates, like E. G. Wood in England and Victor Balagny in
France, the slow acceptance of this still experimental material
by professional photographers and serious amateurs inhibited
both the development of celluloid chemistry and the technology
for its manufacture. When the chronophotographer Étienne-
Jules Marey changed from Eastman paper film to celluloid in
1889, he used either Eastman's nitrocellulose film or strips from
a collodion base sheet made by Victor Balagny that were cut
from photographic plates and never more than 1.10 meters long
(Braun 1992, 153–54). In 1895, as the first generation of movie
inventors turned to solving the problems of projected motion
pictures—and the making of pirate Kinetoscopes—they obtained
longer film supplies from the European Blair Camera Company,
and began as well to press for alternative sources of supply
locally.

The European Blair Camera Company supplied the
Lumière brothers with rolls of strip celluloid throughout 1895 as
they worked on their Cinématographe. But the Lumières, pro-
prietors themselves of one of Europe's largest and most sophisticated photographic plate manufacturing companies, realized
that they would need a dependable source of quality film stock
as part of their moving picture system, and in parallel with the
development of their apparatus began to explore the ways and
means of producing celluloid film, on which they wanted to use
their own excellent photographic emulsion. They turned to Victor Planchon, who had established a small business in Boulogne-
sur-Mer to make the celluloid plates he believed would supplant
glass in photographic work.

The Lumières were already steady customers for Planchon's bulk chemicals, which they used for their famous Eti-
quette Bleu plates. They asked Planchon to prepare some celluloid sheets, but to coat it with their own photosensitive
emulsion. Planchon flowed his celluloid onto large glass sheets
and then added the Lumière emulsion; the full glass sheet, still
with the completed film unstripped, was then transported to
Lyon for the Lumières to test and prepare for their evolving
Cinématographe (Rittaud-Hutinet 1995, 39–43). Meanwhile, the
Lumières investigated the possibilities of obtaining a license to
produce film using the Blair processes, and of receiving bulk

73

FIGURE 13. The emulsion-mixing room at the Lumière factory in Lyon, 1894.

orders from Blair. By late 1895 their experiments with Planchon had run into the same problems the American producers had experienced in the period 1889–92: their emulsion would not adhere properly to Planchon's celluloid base, the consistency and flexibility of the material varied from batch to batch, and there were problems maintaining proper thickness.

As they sought to find their own method of producing celluloid, the Lumières carefully analysed the Blair stock, and wrote to Planchon on January 2, 1896, to say that the stock was still scratching much too easily, and that according to their tests it contained acetanilid: "The proportion is roughly 12% of the total, according to our initial testing. . . . In addition, there would appear to be a very slight quantity of some resinous oil. . . . It might be an idea to adopt this ingredient, since American film is much tougher than your samples" (Rittaud-Hutinet 1995, 86–87). By now, Planchon had agreed to move his factory to Lyon and to establish a new firm that included the Lumières, Jules Carpentier, and others as investors. By 1903 Planchon was managing the Lumière's fifty-acre photochemical plant at Feyzin outside Lyon.

By the end of the century, only a few small companies had joined these pioneering films to supply raw film stock for taking moving pictures or making positive prints for sale to the rapidly expanding business. One of these smaller firms that for a short period was an important supplier of an essential commodity in short supply was established just north of London in the suburban town of Barnet as the Northern Photographic Works by the filmmaker and inventor Birt Acres, who was largely financed by his old associates from Germany, the Stollwerck Chocolate Company (see chapter 5). Another small celluloid manufacturing firm used by Continental filmmakers was the well-established dry-plate manufacturer and photographic supplier Dr. J. H. Smith & Co. of Zurich, Switzerland. In America, the small Goodwin Film & Camera Company in Newark, New Jersey, was active throughout the period, although mostly as a proof of the validity of the Goodwin patents. This company slowly evolved into the later Ansco film manufacturing establishment. The Lumière brothers tried to enter the U.S. market, through a dry plate factory in Burlington, Vermont, but with little success.

Nonetheless, celluloid film became firmly established during the 1890s as the only satisfactory medium for "living pictures," at first in the Edison Kinetoscope and then in the machines of Skladanowsky, Lumière, Paul, Armat, Casler, and many other inventors. It combined toughness, flexibility, and transparency with an ability to hold a photographic emulsion, and in widths ranging from 17.5 mm through 35 mm and up to 70 mm it would hold enough individual photographs for projected moving pictures to allow a minimum of ten or fifteen seconds duration, with a theoretically unlimited maximum duration. With the single exception of glass-plate cinematography for amateur use in the home, there were no serious alternatives to celluloid in motion picture work: the new plastic material was no longer just a substitute for ivory, or an imitation of other natural materials. But when celluloid became a key and central component of movie apparatus, it brought to the movies its flammability and its wide public reputation as a dangerous relative of explosive gun-cotton.

As early as 1875 the *New York Times* had editorialized on the subject of "Explosive Teeth" (September 16, 1895, 4); in its first 36 years in Newark, the Celluloid Manufacturing Company's factory was the site of 39 fires and explosions, which caused at least 9 deaths and 39 injuries (Friedel, 1983, 96). In April 1892, *Scientific American* reported on the ignition of celluloid buttons in a dress after its wearer stood too long near a fireplace (*Scientific American* 66: 208) When celluloid film became an essential component of moving picture exhibitions, it brought into the cinema this reputation for flammability. For both concerned officials and the wider public, it was the flammability of celluloid that was primarily identified with the great tragedy of the Société Charité Maternelle, when fire broke out during a charity ball on May 4, 1897, killing 143 French socialites and members of the aristocracy. The fire was actually caused by the Molteni oxygen-ether limelight, which had gone out and was irresponsibly relit by the projectionists, causing the highly volatile gas to explode; the temporary ballroom structure on the rue Jean Goujon just off the Champs Elysées in Paris was destroyed in minutes. This event, which is also misreported in many later film histories, cemented the images of fire and celluloid film in the public's mind, and was the last crucial "contribution" of celluloid to the early cinema. Before the Charity Bazaar Fire, cinema shows were frequently projected to upper-class audiences and at charitable or fashionable events, such as the screenings at the Paris Opera in January 1896 or those accompanying the 1896 Proms concerts in London (Rossell, 1995, 141, 210n68). Pioneers like Karl Pahl in Berlin and David Devant in London also recall giving cinema shows in private homes during 1896, a longstanding tradition of magic lantern exhibitors (Pahl 1933, 4; Devant 1931, 138). The tragedy of the French charity fire, and its association with the long-established history of celluloid flammability not only hastened the imposition of public-safety control over cinema exhibitions, but also hastened the exit of moving picture shows from early sites like legitimate theaters, concert halls, private homes, and fancy masked balls, relegating it to the more carefree variety theaters, fairgrounds, and market festivals where there was less concern about both fire insurance and fire safety.

The negative connotations of celluloid were a major influence on the development of moving pictures and on the terms under which it was accepted by society. The need for fire security, including enclosed projection booths and multiple exits for the audience, both determined the construction of elaborate travelling fairground exhibition shows and turned the fixed-location cinema toward varieté and vaudeville theatres, slowly moving its focus away from home or personal use and from its early public-house and hotel venues. Flammable celluloid helped moved the cinema into arenas distinct from magic lantern work. Although both media presented, in one aspect, a fire danger through the use of illuminant gases, especially oxy-hydrogen limelight, the variety of illuminant choices and the decades-long experience with magic lantern lamp houses meant that the light source for both magic lantern and cinema projection was considered a danger that could be limited and controlled. In situations where fire danger was considered high, or where the authorities were strict, alternatives such as electric arc lamps could be chosen. In the home or for small rooms, oil lamps or municipal coal gas could be used. But for the cinema there was no alternative to the "explosive" nitrocellulose film, and changing to a safer source of illumination such as electricity did not, in the eyes of many, significantly reduce the danger of setting the celluloid afire.

Although the flammability of nitrate film was recognized from the beginnings of the cinema as an added danger to the already potentially risky business of projecting images, it is interesting to note that when a nonflammable acetate-based celluloid that had been under development by both Eastman and Pathé since 1906 was offered to the market by Eastman in 1908, film producers and exhibitors rejected its use since the old problems of manufacture appeared once again (Jenkins 1975, 288–90). The photographic emulsion did not properly adhere to the safety film base, the material was less tough than flammable film and more liable to scratching and tearing, and the emulsion quality was not considered comparable. Eastman withdrew their safety film from the market in 1911 and it was thereafter used only for home amateur equipment, such as Edison's Projecting Home Kinetoscope of 1912. Flammable nitrate celluloid film remained the industry standard worldwide until the late 1940s.

CHAPTER FIVE

Shaping the Future:
Thomas Alva Edison
and the Kinetoscope

The relationship between the inventor Thomas Alva Edison and moving pictures is problematic. More than seventy-five books have been written about Edison and his work on the electric light and electricity, the phonograph, telegraphy, the telephone, storage batteries, and the dozens of other inventions and technological devices that sprang from his fertile and industrious activity. The standard biographies (Dyer and Martin 1910; Josephson 1959; Conot 1979; Wachhorst 1981) all include a chapter in which Edison is described as the inventor of moving pictures, but almost all lack any perspective on concurrent international developments and are superficial in their handling of the work at Edison's laboratory. Specialist film literature is sharply divided, with some authors celebrating Edison's accomplishments as the sole progenitor of the movies (Ramsaye 1926) and others aggressively denying any significant contributions on Edison's part and attributing the work that came from his West Orange laboratory wholly to his assistant and chief investigator of the moving picture project, W. K. L. Dickson (Hendricks 1961). The best recent accounts (Musser 1990, 1991) are by definition limited to the American scene and do not explore the unusual aspects of Edison's international influence.

Some of the problems involved in assessing Edison's contributions to the invention of moving pictures result from the dubious state of his laboratory records used in later court cases. Some arise from his easy public statements about work in reality not finished that he gave in many newspaper stories and interviews. Other problems appear when the story of the Edison Kinetoscope is dropped from the historical literature as soon as film projection appears on the scene. More problems come from the retrospective shadow cast by Edison's later central role in the moving picture business in the era of the Motion Picture Patents Company (1908–15), which left an indelible impression of continuous leadership by the Wizard of Menlo Park from the first days of the cinema. To begin to unravel the many strands of Edison's involvement with moving pictures, the Kinetoscope must be seen in the context of his other projects at his "invention factory."

In the late 1880s, when initial work on the Kinetoscope began at the West Orange laboratory, Edison had been a full-time professional inventor for twenty years. He worked frequently for major corporations, often under an annual contract, and made many contributions to the development of telegraphy, improved Alexander Graham Bell's telephone, invented an office recording machine he called the phonograph, and developed a practical electric light bulb. Like the other inventors of his day, including Samuel Morse and Cyrus Hall McCormick, Edison watched over his inventions from initial concept to practical solution to commercial manufacturing and sales, frequently establishing affiliated companies to make, install, and operate the devices that flowed from his research work. He was, says Thomas P. Hughes, "a holistic conceptualizer and determined solver of the problems associated with the growth of systems" (Hughes 1983, 18).

Edison described his approach to the electric light bulb, for example, by saying

> It was not only necessary that the lamps should give light and the dynamos generate current, but the lamps must be adapted to the current of the dynamos, and the dynamos must be constructed to give the character of current required by the lamps, and likewise all parts of the system

must be constructed with reference to all other parts, since, in one sense, all the parts form one machine, and the connections between the parts being electrical instead of mechanical. Like any other machine the failure of one part to cooperate properly with the other part disorganizes the whole and renders it inoperative for the purpose intended. The problem then that I undertook to solve was stated generally, the production of the multifarious apparatus, methods and devices, each adapted for use with every other, and all forming a comprehensive system. (Hughes 1983, 22)

Typically, Edison also announced his electrical system prematurely, choosing a a long-standing favorite vehicle, the newspaper columns of the *New York Sun*. On October 20, 1878, he revealed plans for underground electrical distribution in big cities using central generating stations and predicted his light bulb would be cheaper than gas burners and make them obsolete. "He spoke not only of his incandescent lamp," comments Thomas Hughes, "but of other envisaged components of his system, such as meters, dynamos, and distribution mains. In fact, he had no generator, no practical incandescent lamp, much less a developed system of distribution—these were at least a year away. He did, however, have the concept" (Hughes 1983, 32–33).

It was Edison's drive toward an interrelated system that defined his first thoughts on moving pictures, expressed in a clear and memorable catchphrase in the opening lines of his first motion picture caveat of October 1888: "I am experimenting upon an instrument which does for the Eye what the phonograph does for the Ear, which is the recording and reproduction of things in motion, and in such a form as to be both Cheap practical and convenient. This apparatus I call a Kinetoscope 'Moving View'" (Hendricks 1961, 158). When Edison filed this caveat, a confidential document lodged with the patent office that could be used to establish precedence and bar other inventors from entering the same field, his new apparatus was nearly five years away from its first professional demonstration.

The idea of combining the phonograph, Edison's startling device for reproducing speech and music, with a new apparatus for moving views seems so natural a step for the inventor that it is perhaps understandable that in later years he denied discussing a combination of picture and sound with Eadweard Muybridge. The chronophotographer came to Orange, New Jersey, to give a lecture for the New England Society on February 25, 1888, and two days later the pair had a long visit. Edison told a journalist at the time that Muybridge "was conducting a series of experiments recently and had almost perfected a photographic appliance by which he would be enabled to accurately reproduce the gestures and the facial expressions of, for instance, Mr. Blaine in the act of making a speech. . . . He [Muybridge] proposed to Mr. Edison that the phonograph should be used in connection with his invention, and that photographs of Edwin Booth as Hamlet, Lillian Russell in some of her songs, and other artists of note should be experimented with" (Musser 1990, 62).

Fitting the Kinetoscope "Moving View" into his current system, Edison first planned a device using a cylinder the same size as his phonograph, on which some 42,000 tiny images about $1/32$ inches wide, would be fixed in a spiral and viewed through a microscope lens while ear tubes provided the single spectator with the accompanying sound. William Kennedy Laurie Dickson, one of Edison's principle assistants and the laboratory's photography specialist was assigned to the Kinetoscope project, assisted by Charles A. Brown and occasionally by others on the laboratory staff. At first, Dickson poured collodion emulsion over the cylinder to make it photographically sensitive; quickly sheets of John Carbutt's celluloid films were substituted, wrapped around a larger cylinder about $4\frac{1}{2}$ inches in diameter, but the awkward surface still tended to leave the edges of the tiny images out of focus.

When Edison returned to West Orange from a European trip in October 1889 and saw the ambiguous results of the tests, which involved photographs of an employee dressed in white gesturing wildly in front of a black background, the research at the laboratory moved in new directions. As Dickson recalled in several 1894 articles, he abandoned the tiny photographs and substituted

> a series of very much larger impressions affixed to the outer edge of a swiftly rotating wheel, or disk, and supplied with a number of pins, so arranged as to project under the center

of each picture. On the rear of the disk, upon a stand, was placed a Geissler tube, connected with an induction coil, the primary wire of which, operated by the pins, produced a rupture of the primary circuit, which, in its turn, through the medium of the secondary circuit, lighted up the Geissler tube at the precise moment when a picture crossed its range of view. (Hendricks 1961, 84)

This is an accurate description of the second model of the Anschütz Schnellseher, or Tachyscope, which had been reported in the press in Europe and America, and became the cover story of *Scientific American* in November 1889. Gordon Hendricks argues strongly that the Edison laboratory either purchased or themselves built just such an Anschütz machine, which Edison employee Eugene Lauste also remembers seeing in the photographic building at West Orange, a machine that may have been used in an exhibition of Edison's work at the Lenox Lyceum in New York City in April 1890 (Hendricks 1961, 84–92).

In November 1889, Edison drew up a new caveat describing his moving picture work, by now his fourth attempt to protect a possible direction of work at the laboratory. This fourth caveat is based on Edison's ideas after a meeting with Étienne-Jules Marey in Paris, and suggests a Kinetoscope using a single long band of film moving across a viewing aperture. Over the next months, Dickson, assisted now by William Heise, constructed a new camera that used a ³/₄-inch strip of celluloid film running horizontally through the apparatus, as it did in Marey's chronophotographic devices. Unlike Marey, however, Dickson and Heise added a single row of perforations along one side of the film, and produced circular images like those commonly seen in magic lantern slides. By spring 1891, their new design had recorded short films of boxers, gymnasts, and a close view of a man smoking a pipe, all taken against a black background. On May 20, a prototype Kinetoscope viewer using the ³/₄-inch film was shown to a group from the Women's Clubs of America who were meeting in West Orange and being entertained by Mrs. Edison; by August 24, three patents on the apparatus were filed: one for the method of taking and reproducing the pictures (Edison 1891), one for the Kinetograph camera (Edison 1891a), and one for the Kinetoscope viewer (Edison 1891b).

Edison's patents on his Kinetoscope work had an arduous trip through the patent office and only emerged two or more years after they were filed, in much altered form (see Musser 1990, 238–39, and Hendricks 1961, 130–37). Along with the five motion picture caveats reaching back to 1888, they formed the basis of Edison's many later attempts to assert control over the American motion picture business and the very broadly drawn specifications were hotly contested for the next twenty years. The battle over the issuance of these patents also distorted the records of work at the Edison laboratory and the statements both then and later of many participants. As one historian of technology has written, "Patents and patent litigation shape memories so strongly that disinterested accounts based on them cannot be assumed" (Hughes 1983, 110).

Edison's success in persuading the patent office to grant the very broad claims in his original patents, combined with his aggressive use of the legal system to pursue all of the motion picture technologies that appeared throughout 1895 and after, distinguished the American film scene from the one that developed more naturally in Britain, France, and Germany. In his early work in telegraphy, as Edison worked for some of the largest and most competitive American corporations, he was educated in a tough school of late nineteenth-century capitalism. For one example among many, Western Union kept Edison under contract to preserve their competitive advantage in controlling a duplex telegraph, which allowed two messages to be sent simultaneously over the same wire. Western Union president William Orton urged Edison "to invent as many processes as possible [in order] to anticipate other inventors in new modes and also to patent as many combinations as possible." Edison was clear about the assignment, as he later testified that his job was to invent alternative duplexes "as an insurance against other parties using them—other lines" (Israel 1989, 69). Edison learned quickly how best to manipulate the patent system and had the financial strength and juridicial experience to freely invoke the legal system to back up his various claims and maneuvers in the marketplace.

Famously, he did not pursue patents on his Kinetograph camera and Kinetoscope viewer in Europe, later stating that it was a question of expense, a failure that most historians have considered a grievous mistake. But Charles Musser rightly suggests that the very wide claims granted in his American patents would not have been allowed in Britain, France, or Germany (Musser 1990, 71–72, 504n32). Edison and his legal team were certainly well experienced in European patent law through many applications on behalf of other work at the laboratory, and apart from prior claims in Europe from Aimé Augustin le Prince, William Friese Greene, and others, any European impingement on the broad claims granted him in America would have considerably weakened Edison's position at home.

While Edison's patent applications were being negotiated with the patent examiner in Washington, Dickson and Heise continued to search for a practical moving picture system. An order for 1½ inch wide (35 mm) celluloid film 50 feet long was placed with the Eastman Dry Plate Company in November 1891; when the stock arrived, the emulsion separated from its celluloid base and it was unusable, Dickson's first hint of many troubles to come with the physical characteristics of transparent celluloid film (see chapter 4). In moving to film twice as wide as in the horizontal-feed camera, Dickson wanted to strengthen the film band so that it would less easily tear or break; adding a second row of perforations also lessened the tearing of the sprocket holes in the film as it moved intermittently through the camera, now a vertical-feed apparatus. The original intermittent movement for the new camera was provided by a pair of disks set at right angles to each other. One, with a single slot, moved continuously. The second disk was connected to a sprocket wheel moving the film through the camera, and had three protruding teeth bearing on the first disk, one of which dropped through the slot each time it revolved, thereby moving the sprocket intermittently. The apparatus was driven by an electric motor at about forty frames per second, and was far from portable. This camera was developed during summer, 1892, and had produced films by October, when views of men fencing and boxing appeared in *The Phonogram* (Musser 1991, 32).

The Kinetoscope viewer was adapted to the new 35 mm film and found its final design at the same time. Standing four feet high, completely enclosed in a wooden case with a single eye-piece for an individual viewer, the film subject ran through the machinery continuously. It was this continuous movement of the film that required the high shooting speed of around forty frames per second in the camera (the speed varied slightly from subject to subject, and some later films were taken at a slower speed). A horizontal shutter, in the form of a wheel with a single slotted opening ran between the eyepiece and the film, which was joined in a loop forty-two feet long and threaded over storage spools in the case. Again, an electric motor drove the apparatus, as well as powering a shaded electric light bulb beneath the viewing aperture. A spectator viewed the film by transmitted light, one of the advantages of the Blair Camera Company films that were used almost exclusively for Kinetoscope work by Edison and Dickson, since they they had a slightly frosted or translucent celluloid base supplied to Blair by the Celluloid Manufacturing Company of Newark, New Jersey.

The first public professional demonstration of the Kinetoscope was given by Prof. George M. Hopkins at the Brooklyn Institute on May 9, 1893. President of the institute's Department of Physics, he presented an illustrated lecture on the Kinetoscope at the department's monthly meeting, using the famous Choreutoscope images of a dancing skeleton projected by a magic lantern to explain the essential principle of the new apparatus. The evening's finale was an opportunity for the audience to see the single completed Kinetoscope and the films *Blacksmith Scene*, showing a blacksmith and his two helpers photographed in front of a black background hammering on an anvil, and *Horse Shoeins*. The films were shot in the Black Maria, a photographic studio for Kinetoscope work at the Edison laboratory begun in December 1892 and finished in February of the next year, which provided an electrically serviced enclosed building for taking films by direct sunlight: the building featured an overhead skylight and could rotate on a graphite center to follow the sun across the sky. As reported in *Scientific American* on May 20, 1893, Hopkins called the Kinetoscope "a refinement of Plateau's phenakistoscope or the Zootrope" and also noted its debt to "the work accomplished by Muybridge and Anschuetz, who very successfully photographed animals in motion, and to Demeny, who produced an instrument called the phonoscope." Hopkins emphasized that in its fully developed form (not yet available) the Kinetoscope was an apparatus for projecting moving pictures on a screen that would be accompa-

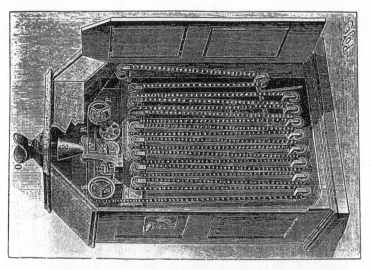

FIGURE 14. The production model of the Kinetoscope viewer of Thomas Edison and William Kennedy Laurie Dickson, 1894, with its endless loop of 35mm wide film.

nied by sound synchronized with a phonograph (the entire account is reprinted in Musser 1991, 36–38).

Over the next year, film production began in earnest at West Orange, with Dickson and Heise filming Edison employee Fred Ott sneezing, a Highland dance, an organ grinder, amateur gymnasts, and a number of vaudeville and variety performers, including strongman Eugene Sandow, Professor Harry Welton's wrestling dog and boxing cats, the dancer Annabelle Whitford essaying her butterfly dance, members of Buffalo Bill's Wild West Show and scenes from the musical comedy *The Milk White Flag*. Charles Musser described the Edison filming methods as owing much "to nineteenth-century photographic practices and, most important, to the phonograph. Phonograph performers were usually placed in a recording studio that isolated them from miscellaneous sounds. Correspondingly, the Maria, with its black walls, eliminated extraneous visual distractions. This dark background also placed its subjects in bold relief in a manner that recalls Eadweard Muybridge's serial views" (Musser 1990, 78). Throughout the life of the Kinetoscope, the choice of film subjects also echoed Edison's earlier phonograph subjects. The Edison cylinder recordings are dominated by march music by John Phillip Sousa and others, by middle-class "potted palm" music popular in the hotel courts of the day, and by odd novelty banjo and harmonica players. Similarly, the films that emerged from the unnatural setting of the Black Maria were drawn from Broadway plays, provided a tamed and commercialized vision of the Wild West, or recorded strange novelties like a cock fight. Not until May 1896 did Edison complete a portable camera that William Heise could use outside the Black Maria studio.

The first group of Kinetoscopes was ready for sale in April 1894 and was delivered to a syndicate including Alfred O. Tate, Edison's former business manager; Thomas Lombard and Erastus Benson, who were active in the phonograph business; Norman C. Raff and Frank R. Gammon; and Andrew Holland. A storefront Kinetoscope parlor was opened by the Holland Brothers at 1155 Broadway, New York City, on April 14, 1895, and found instant success with the public. Holland opened a second parlor in Chicago in mid-May, and a third was opened by Peter Bacigalupi in San Francisco on June 1. At first sold singly to a wide range of entrepreneurs, amusement parks, and other customers, by the summer of 1894 Edison had rationalized his system for promoting the Kinetoscope, with Raff & Gammon organizing the Kinetoscope Company to control sales in the United States and Canada, and former phonograph agent Frank Z. Maguire and Wall Street lawyer Joseph D. Baucus obtaining the rights to the Kinetoscope overseas, incorporating as the Continental Commerce Company. From early in his career Edison had been an inventor of devices for business organizations, and habitually "focused his efforts on producing machines for business markets and avoided marketing products to the masses" (Carlson 1992, 181). His Kinetoscope agents, who guaranteed a certain number of purchases from Edison and then took the risk in selling them to showmen, repeated a pattern that was typical not only for Edison, who replicated his experiences with his phonograph and electrical enterprises, but also for other inventor-entrepreneurs with new products like the Celluloid Manufacturing Company and later the Lumière brothers in France.

The rapid deployment of the Kinetoscope across the United States was duplicated in Europe. The Paris concession went to Michel and Eugène Werner, who opened ten machines at 20 boulevard Poissonière, not far from the Musée Grevin, October 1, 1894. The concession for Germany went to the Deutsch-Österreichischen-Edison-Kinetoskop-Gesellschaft, whose main financial backer was the Stollwerck Company, chocolate manufacturers who were already involved with Demenÿ's Phonoscope. Maguire and Baucus themselves opened the first parlor in England at 70 Oxford Street, London, on October 17, and the Kinetoscope opened in Sydney, Australia on November 30, and in the Netherlands on December 27, in Amsterdam. In big cities around the world and in the small towns across America that were increasingly serviced by Raff & Gammon, the Kinetoscope was received with astonishment and wonder. The correspondent of the London *Daily Graphic* wrote "hardly ever has anything more striking and pretty been shown than the kinetoscopes which Mr Maguire, acting as the European representative of Mr Edison, exhibited at the conversazione last night in Oxford Street" (October 18, 1894, 8) and C. A. P. Ivens noted in the *Nijmeegsche Courant* that the "uniqueness of the Kinetoscope is the naturalism of its movements, its smooth transition between different phases, through which the senses receive an impression of continuous action" (May 6, 1895).

The quick dissemination of the Kinetoscope, an expensive machine selling at first for $350 each (prices had dropped to about $150 in June 1895), is evidence of the eagerness with which both showmen and audiences awaited any device that could reproduce "living pictures," especially if it had the magic name of Edison attached. Similar excitement had attended Demenÿ's initial exhibition of the Phonoscope, when he was besieged by the "Barnums" who wanted to exploit the machine in 1892 (chapter 3), and accompanied the introduction of the Schnellseher as Anschütz received enquiries from Brazil, North Africa, and across Europe soliciting information (Rossell 1996a). Any kind of moving picture, any new "wonder apparatus," was noticed and quickly sought by potential operators who saw opportunities in exhibiting it to the public.

In such an atmosphere, the long eleven months between the Kinetoscope's demonstration at the Brooklyn Institute and the opening of the first Kinetoscope parlor in New York was an unusual and unnatural delay. The Kinetoscope was widely publicized from at least May 1893; why did Edison order only twenty-five of the machines in June 1893, and why did it take until March 1894 to make them? Why did Edison let this manufacture slide for so long? By doing so he missed exhibiting the Kinetoscope at the Columbian Exhibition in Chicago, an important venue for introducing new machinery where Muybridge showed his Zoöpraxiscope and lectured throughout the fair and where the Anschütz electrical Schnellseher was also on display.

Edison must have received the same blizzard of enquiries that reached Demenÿ and Anschütz. At this particular moment in the earliest days of moving pictures, a delay of eleven months in marketing a finished apparatus that had already been in development for some four years was an eternity. Within the context of his growing electrical business, and the intense research on ore-milling that occupied most of the attention at West Orange, the Kinetoscope was not a major project for Edison, but still the long gap between demonstration and availability is unusual. Perhaps Edison saw no "system" into which the Kinetoscope would fit, and was trying in some way to think out a more practical use for it. When he did finally begin to supply Kinetoscopes

to Raff & Gammon in the United States and Maguire and Baucus overseas, Edison slowly transferred more and more respon-
sibility for the apparatus to his agents. Both firms began to pay
the costs of making new Kinetoscope productions, and one of
Raff & Gammon's clients, the Kinetoscope Exhibition Company, organized by Otway Latham with his father, brother, and
Enoch J. Rector, probably suggested expanding the capacity of
the Kinetoscope so it could show longer films (Musser 1990, 82).
The larger capacity machines could hold 150 feet of film,
enough for a shortened one-minute round of boxing, a special
interest of Latham and his partners, when the speed was low-
ered to around thirty frames per second. They quickly produced
a six-round fight between Michael Leonard and Jack Cushing at
the Black Maria in June 1894, and a second fight between heavyweight champion James Corbett and Peter Courtney in September, which remained a popular staple of early film exhibition
through 1897.

In both Europe and America, sales of the Kinetoscope were
brisk until the spring of 1895, but suffered a permanent decline
in summer. Two problems arose: competitors making their own
kinetoscope viewers, in several forms, and a scarcity of new film
productions. Both issues brought new competitors into the marketplace. In America, an alternative kinetoscope was made by
Charles E. Chinnock from late 1894. The Chinnock machine,
which was patented in Great Britain by James Edward Hough
(Hough 1894), held film wound in a spiral around a drum turned
by a handle, similar to an alternative design included in
Demenÿ's Phonoscope patent (Demenÿ 1892). The drum was
mounted on a helical screw, so that the wound length of film
passed a stationary viewing aperture as it revolved. Installed in
bars and cafés in New York, Chinnock was able to supply his
own films of boxers, a cock fight, a blacksmith scene, and skirt
dancers that were conscious imitations of the Edison productions. Although Chinnock claimed to have supplied his film
camera to both Hough in England and to Michel Werner in
France (then Edison's Paris concessionaire), corroborating evidence for his claim has not yet been found.

The major European competition for the Kinetoscope came
from direct copies of the Edison machine made by the electrical
engineer and scientific instrument maker Robert W. Paul, who

found that the apparatus was not patented in England. Paul had been asked to make additional kinetoscopes by the owners of at least three legitimate Edison machines, George Georgiades and George Tragides, so they could expand their kinetoscope parlors in London. Paul sold the two exhibitors his first reproduction kinetoscopes but quickly entered the business himself, exhibiting his own machines at the Crystal Palace in south London, and selling as well to other clients, including the phonograph exhibitor Charles Pathé in Paris. Needing a source of films for his kinetoscopes, Paul began to consider making a camera, and a mutual friend named Henry Short introduced him to the photographer Birt Acres, then manager of the Barnet works just north of London for the photographic manufacturers Elliott and Son. Like many of the early alliances at the beginning of moving picture experimentation, including Armat and Jenkins or Joly and Pathé, their partnership was brief if significant, with many later years of recrimination and false reminiscence that have muddied the historical record. Paul's account is best known, and was in print in one of the first film histories (Talbot 1912, 33–43): he became known as "Daddy Paul," the founder of the British film industry, and remained active in film historical circles until his death in 1943. But the recent discovery of contemporary documentation at the Stollwerck Archive in Cologne (by both Hauke Lange-Fuchs and Martin Loiperdinger) lends much credence to Acres's account of the partnership. What is clear is that Paul had no photographic background, although he was an experienced manufacturer of electrical instruments. Acres, on the other hand, had no business sense but in addition to his photographic background had early on a vision of moving pictures.

The two men met on February 4, 1895, and Acres signed an agreement with Paul to design a camera that Paul would manufacture in his workshops and that would then be used to supply films for the Paul kinetoscopes. Acres went to work right away, and the first Paul-Acres camera was working by March 29, when Paul sent clips of the 35 mm results, a film of Henry Short in front of Acres's cottage in Barnet, to Thomas Edison in New Jersey, suggesting that he could supply additional films for the Kinetoscope. The next day, Acres and Paul filmed *Oxford and Cambridge Boat Race,* and by the beginning of June several more films had been completed, including *The Arrest of a Pickpocket, The Comic Shoeblack, The Boxing Kangaroo*, and a film of the 1895 English Derby, which was recently rediscovered by the National Film and Television Archive in London. The camera that was used for these pioneering films was patented by Acres alone in May 1895 as a combination camera and projector, and featured an unusual intermittent movement where a clamp operated by a camshaft pressed momentarily against the film during its exposure; a roller tensioned by a spring bore on the film and absorbed some of the length of film as it was momentarily stopped by the clamp (Acres 1895a). According to Paul's later account, this awkward intermittent was replaced "after a few weeks" by a seven-sided Maltese cross arrangement that produced better results. But precisely which of the partners was responsible for the improvement is unclear, since Paul also contended that while Acres contributed some ideas to the initial venture together, it was largely his own construction and property. Yet a letter written by Acres to Ludwig Stollwerck in Cologne on August 6, 1895, just nine weeks or so after the partnership broke up, states flatly that Paul had indeed made the camera, but to Acres's original designs, and that after their split Paul then charged Acres £30 for his work on it, which Acres paid in full (Acres 1895). Paul's contention that the camera was improved "in a few weeks" with a Maltese cross may be another case of faulty memory, for the German patent on the Acres camera from August 1895 shows the same pressure-plate intermittent, although now improved by a better arrangement of tensioning springs and a more responsive and precise pressure plate (Acres 1895b).

After the partnership acrimoniously broke up, the two men reacted very differently to the opportunities provided by moving pictures. Paul stayed in the electrical instrument business, continuing to make and exhibit his kinetoscopes, but made no new films during the remainder of the year. He also applied for a patent, never issued, inspired by H. G. Wells's story "The Time Machine," which envisioned a complex visual environment including films, slides, and theatrical constructions where an audience would "travel" through exotic scenes of the past or future, something on the order of the later Hale's Tours shows. In very late 1895 or early 1896, inspired by the Lumière Cinématographe, he quickly built an important projector (see chapter 7) which was first shown publicly in London in February 1896 (Barnes 1976, 41).

Acres, on the other hand, left his job at the dry plate factory and plunged wholly into moving picture work. He improved his camera, attempted to make a projector for screen presentation of moving pictures, and found backing from the Stollwerck chocolate manufacturers, who were already involved with the Demenÿ Phonoscope and the Edison Kinetoscope in Germany. For Stollwerck, he filmed the opening of the Kiel Canal in June 1895 and made additional films in Hamburg and Berlin. A Stollwerck agent, Paul Müller, patented the improved Acres camera in Germany, and Acres agreed to make at least five more cameras for use by Stollwerck agents, including J. Hamann in Hamburg and H. O. Foersterling in Berlin, to make films for the Stollwerck kinetoscopes (Lange-Fuchs 1995, 40, 62). By January 1996, Acres was demonstrating his projection apparatus, still using a clamping intermittent that was vaguely reminiscent of Marey's 1890 design, in London and other towns in England. But, undercapitalized and inattentive to business matters, he never really turned his very early experience with moving pictures for the kinetoscope into a leading position in the new world of screen practice, remaining a supplier of raw film stock and laboratory services until 1909. That passage from peep show to projection would be successfully negotiated by a group in the United States inspired by the Edison Kinetoscope, including Harry Marvin, Herman Casler, Elias Koopman, and W. K. L. Dickson.

Edison's house photographer and chief Kinetoscope experimenter W. K. L. Dickson met Harry Marvin during an earlier Edison assignment when he worked on laying underground electrical cables in Brooklyn, New York, in 1884. The two became friends, and vacationed together in 1888; by the summer of 1891 or 1892, Marvin had introduced Dickson to his colleague at the C. E. Lipe machine shop in Syracuse, New York, Herman Casler (Hendricks 1964, 6–7). By 1893 Casler and Dickson had devised a miniature camera in the form of a large pocket-watch called the Photoret, which took six hexagonal images 13 mm across on a 1¾ inch disk of celluloid film (Coe 1978, 61; Casler 1893). The amusing detective camera, on which Casler and Dickson shared the royalties, was marketed by the Magic Introduction Company of New York, owned by Elias B. Koopman. This was the circle of four friends and associates who worked well together and prepared to work on a new form of kinetoscope in the last part of 1894, calling themselves K.C.M.D. after their initials. The suggestion for a moving picture device seems to have come from Dickson, who wanted to market another novelty for home consumption, an alternative kinetoscope based on the principle

FIGURE 15. An early model Mutoscope of Herman Casler, from 1897.

of the flip books that had been popular toys since at least 1868 (Linnett 1868). Dickson's idea was to mount individual photographs in series in a box so that they could be flicked through and leave the viewer with an impression of motion. The idea was simplicity itself, a kind of miniaturized Kinetoscope without the batteries, without the electric motor, the light, the flammable celluloid, the delicate mechanics, the high price. But from this simple beginning came the only machine that gave real competition to the Edison Kinetoscope (and that outlived it by decades), and an alternative motion picture system that would be Edison's major rival in the moving picture business.

The Mutoscope, as the four partners called their machine, was ready in the autumn of 1895 and a patent application was filed on November 14. This application described, in reality, novelties for Koopman's Magic Introduction Company. The application was divided and three patents resulted: one for a hand-held peep-box where the images were arranged on a sliding tray inside the viewer (Casler 1895); one for a tabletop Mutoscope with a wheel of images turned by a heavy bent crank geared directly to the hub of the wheel (Casler 1895a), and the third for a flat open shoebox Mutoscope with the cards raked by a small stick (Marvin 1895). A later patent (Casler 1896c) confirms the wide range of K.C.M.D.'s products, describing a hand-held device looking like a medium-sized paint brush where the photographic cards were flicked by an ingeniously shaped bent wire crank running through the handle and around to the top of the cards; a device with the cards arranged on a long flexible band; and the tabletop Mutoscope with several improvements to its mechanics and to the fixing of the cards to the wheel. The next task for the group was to make a camera that could supply photographs for their various peep-show exhibition devices, and here again Dickson's experience and advice proved crucial.

In the first half of 1895 most of the group rearranged their lives. Marvin left the C. E. Lipe company and founded a machine shop in the small town of Canastoda in upstate New York's Finger Lakes region, Casler joined him there as superintendant, and Dickson left the Edison workshops in West Orange. As a result, the development of the group's camera took most of the year. The mechanism for their camera was tested in February 1895 with paper, in June with film, and a boxing match was photographed on August 5 (Musser 1990, 145–46). The technology employed both avoided Edison's (and Dickson's) prior work and was particularly adapted to the group's flip-card exhibition devices. It used unperforated film $2^3/4$ inches, or 70 mm wide, that was moved intermittently through the machine by a "broken roller" or "gripper" friction movement, with the works driven by an electric motor. In this type of intermittent, the film ran between two synchronously driven rollers with a portion of their surface cut away: the film was therefore at rest for exposure in the gate momentarily, and then a new frame was drawn into position through the friction applied when the two extended stubs of the roller came together on each revolution of the cut-away wheels. Unless this intermittent movement was used as an element within a sophisticated film driving and tensioning system, as it later was in the Biograph camera and projector of K.C.M.D., it did not produce reliably exact placement of individual images on the film band. Since these early images were intended to be cut up and printed on flip cards, however, the alternative movement proved perfectly adequate to its purposes, and the camera was also equipped with a punch, or perforator, that incised two circular perforations while each exposure was being taken, which registered the frames for printing on Mutoscope cards. The large size of the image produced by the wide 70 mm film was also particularly appropriate to the Mutoscope where they would be seen as a directly viewed positive prints.

Like the contemporaneous moving picture experiments of the Latham family and the Lambda Company that he also advised (see pp. 123–27), W. K. L. Dickson's participation in K.C.M.D. was a significant one, and he emerges from the early period of American moving picture invention as its central inventive figure, if one who has been little studied. His responsibilities for the day-to-day development of the Edison Kinetoscope and Kinetograph, his concurrent surreptitious advice to two teams of potential competitors, and his gruff break with Edison in April 1895 after the tough new business manager William Gilmore joined Edison to reinvigorate his flagging commercial enterprises, made Dickson an ambiguous figure for later historians. To Edison loyalists he was disreputable and infamous, while others saw him as a repressed talent brimming with ideas crucial to the progress of the moving image. Dickson's own statements and writings over a long period of time are also unclear on the issues of loyalty and deception. What can be learned from a closer look at Dickson's situation?

In the machine-shop culture of the day, it was common for a skilled mechanic to hire out to other entrepreneurs while remaining an employee of a particular shop, just as it was common practice for an employer to, as Edison frequently did, use "inside contracts" with special payments to his mechanics for manufacturing a small batch of devices or for assembling a particularly skillful apparatus. Dickson, indeed, seems to have received either extra pay or some kind of royalty on part of his Kinetoscope work while he was at West Orange. Any senior machine shop craftsman at this time had considerable freedom of action in determining his working day and pace; Edison's own working atmosphere preserved many of these traditional freedoms for employees, although not all of them. This machine-shop culture "gave individuals the opportunity to hire out the means of production, including tools, supplies, and labor. . . . These practices fostered individual initiative and encouraged entrepreneurial activities on the part of the skilled mechanics who worked there" (Millard 1989, 52–53). As the initial Mutoscope patents clearly show, the devices Dickson and his friends were developing were toys and novelties, supported by Koopman's Magic Introduction Company. This work was decisively differentiated from the big-business atmosphere that Dickson found at West Orange, with its giant electrical enterprises and massive investment in iron ore milling experiments (which Dickson also supervised). The expensive and intricate Kinetoscope, with its international franchises, its own production studio, and the resources of Edison's reputation and laboratory behind it was not at all comparable to hand-held or tabletop illusions turned by a handle. The later prominence of American Mutoscope and Biograph Company (AM&B) as a major Edison rival, and the longevity of the Mutoscope as a popular twentieth-century viewer cannot be retrospectively applied to the story of Dickson setting out with a few friends to make another novelty product like the Photoret camera during his last year of employment by Edison.

Dickson's involvement with the Lathams is perhaps more problematic, especially since the Edison records are so fragmentary and incomplete regarding any work on moving picture projection at the laboratory, giving only vague and confused evidence that any experimentation in this direction was undertaken at all. Edison many times rejected developing projection apparatus on commercial grounds once the Kinetoscope was in production, and Dickson may have decided, in his own self-interest since he became a partner in Lambda while still working for Edison, that this, too, was a decisively different initiative than any that he could possibly take up at West Orange. Edison certainly thought his employee disloyal, and regardless of any machine-shop traditions he was certainly possessive about any and all ideas generated by his workers at his laboratory. Was Dickson really so committed to moving picture work that he risked both disfavor and dismissal (which ultimately came) to participate in two outside ventures? Was he frustrated by Edison's blindness to the potentials of moving picture work? Or was he an opportunist who had no respect for his employer?

Edison certainly seems to have had hardly any understanding of, or any sympathy with, the rambunctious and anarchic entertainment industry of the era. The technological frame in which he was most deeply embedded was one of large corporate enterprises involved in fully controlling the technology of systems: the telegraph, electrical power generation and distribution, efficient mining processes. Although a populist figure personally, and a witty and enthusiastic subject for journalists of the day, Edison had neither time nor patience for entertaining diversions; his work was useful, not playful. He conceived of his phonograph as a machine for business dictation and office use, stubbornly trying to market it as a practical aid to businessmen and only reluctantly acceding to its incarnation as a purveyor of entertainment. Alfred O. Tate recalled of the phonograph that Edison was unhappy at its use for entertainment purposes, since that "was associated in his mind with the musical boxes so highly popular during the early Victorian era and broadly classified as 'toys.' . . . [H]e regarded the exploitation of this field as undignified and disharmonious with the more serious objectives of his ambition. He dedicated his life to the production of useful inventions. Devices designed for entertainment or amusement did not in his judgment fall within this classification" (1938, 302).

Edison similarly had little confidence in his Kinetoscope, in part because he could think of no practical businesslike use for it. He wrote to Eadweard Muybridge in 1894 that "I am very doubtful if there is any commercial feature in it & fear that they will not earn their cost. These Zoetropic devices are of too sentimental a character to get the public to invest in" (Carlson 1992, 184). Edison's Kinetoscope business initially returned his costs as some 900 machines were produced. But he had no sense of urgency—no sense of timeliness and prompt response to public interest that is the essential characteristic of a showman. Surrounded since his youth by big businessmen, committed to the creation of technological systems, satisfied that manufacturing was his economic foundation, and convinced that his control of patents meant control of the progress of this new industry, Edison's inability to see the potential of the Kinetoscope or its next simple and logical step was a missed opportunity for the visionary inventor. Like Marey in France, he was a dedicated scientist who had no inclusion in any technological frame that embraced optics, the magic lantern, projected narratives, showmanship, or entertainment. Not only was nothing in Edison's past linked to Charles Musser's "history of screen practice," his outlook was also one where large enterprises were able successfully to control the introduction and diffusion of technology. This, too, was a far different world from the highly individual, scrappy, and seemingly anarchic practices of entertainers and showmen. Edison's one idea was memorably simple, and deceptively captivating: to make an instrument that would "do for the Eye what the phonograph does for the ear." Beyond this striking phrase, Edison seemed to have no idea of what to do with the machine he successfully created. In April 1900, in the face of steeply declining profits and rapidly increasing competition, Edison agreed to sell all of his motion picture interests to the American Mutoscope & Biograph Company, an arrangement that fell through only when AM&B was unable to raise financing for the $500,000 purchase (Musser 1990, 283).

If ever a technological frame became a technological jail, it was in the case of Edison and the Kinetoscope. The potential of the Kinetoscope lay primarily in exactly what Edison said the Kinetoscope was to become, but never actually accomplished: the projection of moving pictures onto a screen. This was a failure of vision, not of Edison's ability to construct the appropriate apparatus, for there is no evidence that his laboratory undertook any serious work on projection until well after many others had achieved and substantively exploited that crucial breakthrough. And by then the always fast-moving entertainment world had left him behind. He would end up fighting the rest of the movie industry that sprang up around him in the courts, an arena he understood well and was fully prepared to use to maximum advantage. But it was a defensive maneuver, by definition slow, costly, and complex. Through the courts he greatly influenced the course of moving pictures in America, but his legal finesse, no matter his later passing attempt to control the young industry through the Motion Picture Patents Company, or his standing as a symbol of the American invention of moving pictures, left him removed from the energetically progressive world of moving pictures in their crucial first years of technological innovation and stabilization. Failing to seize the initiative spawned by the Kinetoscope, he and his companies contributed neither leadership nor innovation to the new industry. Compared with many lesser-known figures—even in the first years of the movies—Edison and his companies always needed to be taken into consideration (those patents) but they and he were always somewhat aloof, never participating significantly in the stabilization of the technology or the creation of film language. He had the right idea, but the work was left to others, just as the essential work on the Kinetoscope at his facilities in West Orange was left to W. K. L. Dickson.

CHAPTER SIX

Seeking an Answer: Out of the Lantern Tradition

While W. K. L. Dickson guided Edison's peep-show Kineto-scope through its long period of gestation, many other experimenters were working on the direct projection of serial images. The principles involved were well known, with the Phenakisto-scope and Zoetrope having reproduced moving pictures for decades, at first with drawn and then with photographic images. The problems of reaching a screen with living pictures were largely mechanical, a search for the combination of moving parts, optics, and photographic materials that would produce an integrated system whereby a minimum of sixteen images per second could be moved past the projection aperture of a device to give an illusion of continuous movement.

Members of several key social groups were involved in this search for projected images, including magic lantern manufacturers and suppliers, photographic manufacturers, specialized instrument makers, photographers, magic lantern exhibitors, panorama and diorama entrepreneurs, science journalists, magicians, entertainment impresarios, and professional inventors. While members of each group made contributions to the extended process of the invention of the cinema over the decade from 1888 through 1898, as will be seen, what is remarkable about the end of the nineteenth century is that there were self-contained dynamics and logical developments within each group that pressed simultaneously toward the realization of moving pictures. The areas of overlap and confluence between these groups forms the arena for Musser's "history of screen practice" (1990, 16–54). The transformation of these traditions of screen practice through new technological apparatus, particularly the screen projection of moving pictures on flexible celluloid film, is the birth of the cinema. This was at first a cinema with an inherited repertoire and an inherited pattern of exhibition. Only later, after about 1903, did this first multifaceted cinema become itself the foundation for a later mass medium that would come to have such an impact on the twentieth century.

The holder of the first British patent for a moving picture device, and one of the most intriguing figures of an era full of mysteries, had an impeccable pedigree as a member of this pioneering group of experimenters. Louis Aimé Augustin Le Prince was taught photography by J. L. M. Daguerre, a family friend. He established a school of applied art in Leeds, England, and was the manager of a group of artists in New York City who painted large circular panoramas for exhibition in New York, Washington, Chicago, and elsewhere (an informative biography is Rawlence 1990). At some time after 1881, when he moved his family to New York, he began experimental work on moving picture machines, patenting his results in 1888 in America, Britain, and France (Le Prince 1888a, 1888b, 1888c). Since his single-lens apparatus was disallowed in America, that patent describes only apparatus with multiple lenses, illustrating a machine Le Prince developed in 1887 with sixteen lenses, but the British and French patents allowed the Le Prince single-lens design. Le Prince had two single-lens cameras by the summer of 1888, using an intermittently moving take-up spool to move the unperforated bands of Eastman paper stripping film through the apparatus. Three sets of images taken with these cameras are preserved at the Science Museum, London, and are evidence that Le Prince was able to record images at somewhere between twelve and twenty pictures per second. The most famous of these images, twenty frames showing traffic on Leeds Bridge, taken from an upper window of the Hick Brothers hardware store around October 1888, is a subject that is strikingly reminiscent of many early films before the turn of the century, with passing wagons and street traffic giving life to the midday scene.

Le Prince's unperforated paper bands meant that his images had to be reprinted if they were to be used in projection. He devised a three-lens "deliverer," or projector, that used individual glass slides prepared from his serial pictures. The slides were fixed on three separate fiber belts that were moved intermittently through the apparatus, apparently by a Maltese Cross arrangement. The design of this projector was inferred from dissolving magic lantern practice, with an image from each of the three bands alternately positioned for projection to the screen, reducing flicker; three bands were necessitated by the weight and consequent inertia of the heavy glass slides as Le Prince attempted to move them into position quickly enough to produce the sixteen images per second that would provide a continuous impression of movement on the screen. The awkwardness of this whole arragement led Le Prince to work on a single-lens projector that had an equally impractical spirally fed arrangement for the slides. He seems to have turned to experimenting with celluloid bands in 1889, but the results of his attempts at projection remain uncertain. The story is further confused by the existence of an odd document signed by Ferdinand Mobisson, the director of the Opéra Garnier in Paris, and notarized by the mayor of the IXth Arrondissement of Paris, Lesage: in this document, signed March 30, 1890, and notarized June 30, 1890, Mobisson certifies that on March 30th he was given a demonstration of living pictures by Le Prince at his office.

Six months after this demonstration, Le Prince boarded a train in Dijon, on his way to Paris with his latest improved apparatus, and was never again seen. Searches by English and French detectives turned up no clues to his disappearance. The enigma of Le Prince contains many elements common to other inventors of the period, and illustrates the many pitfalls facing the proposers of new apparatus. Especially in his projection devices, which have not survived, Le Prince drew on magic lantern practice, locating the site of moving pictures within the double-image systems of dissolving magic lantern apparatus. This double-system approach also had the advantage of allowing the mechanics of the whole machine to operate at "half speed," that is, some eight images per second for each of its doubled elements, which taken together produced on the screen the required minimum of sixteen images necessary for the illusion of continuous movement. On the one hand, a "half speed" apparatus was desirable given the weight and awkwardness of moving glass slides quickly, and on the other hand it offered less strain, and consequently less tearing and breakage, for experimenters working in the less robust medium of celluloid.

The crucial disallowance of a single-lens apparatus in the American patent cleared the way for Edison's later patent for the Kinetograph camera, but this decision by the patent examiners, seen retrospectively, also highlights the difficulties of patentees (and particularly their lawyers) in clearly explaining the workings of their equipment and in distinguishing it from proposals that had received earlier protection in the patent office. The surviving three films are evidence of Le Prince's actual accomplishments, and his steady work on moving pictures between 1881 and his disappearance in 1890 place him among a small group of visionaries, like the chronophotographers Ottomar Anschütz and Georges Demenÿ, who had the imagination and foresight to clearly envision the projection of life-sized moving pictures as a new medium for entertainment and documentation. While modern scholarship has slowly recognized and enlarged the reputation of Le Prince, another such visionary has seen his accomplishments at first hugely fêted and then wholly demolished: the Bath photographer William Friese Greene.

Although having little involvement with the cinema since before the turn of the century, when William Friese Greene died of a heart attack during a film industry meeting in 1921, the dramatic event fixed him for half a century in the British imagination as "the first inventor" of "commercial kinematography," to quote his imposing gravestone. The subject of a lauditory biography by Ray Allister, and then the central figure of *The Magic Box*, a 1951 film celebrating the birth of moving pictures made for the Festival of Britain, Friese Greene was the recipient of a populist hagiography surpassed only by that of the multifaceted Thomas Edison. The publication of a scrupulously researched article by Brian Coe in 1962 finally brought the inconsistencies and inflated claims about an energetic and fanciful character back to earth, although by then much of the Friese Greene legend had been embedded in the historical literature (see Coe 1962; Allister 1948).

Friese Greene was born in 1855 in Bristol and left school to apprentice with a local photographer. He established his own studio for photographic portraits in Bath, and by 1877 operated two additional studios in Bristol and another in Plymouth. He moved to London in 1885 and opened two photographic studios in partnership with Esmé Collings, adding several additional locations to the successful chain during the next six years. It was in London, where he joined the Photographic Society of Great Britain (predecessor to the Royal Photographic Society) and became an active participant in its Technical Meeting, that Friese Greene first began to show a string of new devices and generate a portfolio of comments on his work in the photographic press. Like Edison, Friese Greene was capable of handily announcing dreams as if they were accomplishments, but unlike the genial American he had no substantive track record of accomplishments in other fields that would reinforce his photographic claims, and he often plunged into wildly fantastic propositions.

It was a scientific instrument maker in Bath, John Arthur Roebuck Rudge, who sparked Friese Greene's interest in moving pictures when the two met about 1880. In parallel with his scientific profession, Rudge was an active entertainer who earned the nickname "The Wizard of the Magic Lantern" for his advanced lantern shows, which emphasized a variety of clever constructions to give the impression of movement on the screen, including the Choreutoscope and the Ross Wheel of Life. In the early 1880s he devised a special lantern with seven slides mounted around its circumference and a scissors-like shutter of ground glass for quickly and smoothly changing pictures, and sold one to Friese Greene, who demonstrated it from 1885 as his own invention. Rudge next produced a lantern with four converging lenses that projected a special slide with four sequenced portraits; a single shutter in front of the lenses quickly blended the four images into a single impression of a changing facial expression. Friese Green was the subject of one of these portrait slides, and again demonstrated the invention at photographic societies in London and elsewhere. Another Rudge device of 1888 combined two lanterns each fitted with an endless chain of glass slides linked by metal rings. Operated by a clockwork mechanism driven by a heavy weight, the dissolving lantern system projected images of changing facial expressions giving an illusion of movement. It was for this device that Friese Greene and the civil engineer Mortimer Evans designed and patented a camera capable of taking no more than four or five pictures per second (Friese Greene and Evans 1889).

By 1890, Rudge had produced another new device based on dissolving magic lantern practice that had two lenses and two rotating disks, each of which held seven pictures projected alternately in quick succession, but by now Friese Greene had met and begun to work with Frederick Varley, a London engineer whose hobby was photography. Varley had applied for a patent on March 26, 1890, for an "adjustable displacement lever" that would intermittently move a film band forward in a camera "for obtaining good negatives sufficiently near each other in time to convey the idea of life and motion when successive positives from them are projected at the same speed upon a screen by means of a suitable lantern" (Varley 1890, 1). The patent described two devices, a twin-lens camera that took sequential stereoscopic photographs on Eastman celluloid film 6³/₄ inches wide with images 3 inches square, and a single-lens camera using the same film. Both devices could be used to project translucent positive films. Friese Greene demonstrated and worked with this Varley camera through 1891, and the two occasionally presented it together, for instance, at the London and Provincial Photographic Association on November 27, 1890.

The next year, 1891, Friese Greene was declared bankrupt, and all of his apparatus was apparently sold; he disappeared from view until 1896, with the exception of an 1893 patent for a camera that in overall design and with its odd lever intermittent movement is remarkably similar to Varley's 1890 apparatus. Although his technical accomplishments were largely the work of others, Friese Greene was an incessant publicist for moving pictures. The reports of his various demonstrations are packed with enthusiasm for "exhibiting a more life-like effect upon the screen," or using a phonograph "fitted up in conjunction with the lantern, [so that] the image on the screen might be made to appear to talk," or contending that "we may soon have such lantern exhibitions as continuous representations of street life from a given point" (Coe 1962, 93–94). To the photographic press, Friese Greene had become by 1889 "well known as an experimental photographer and lanternist" and when Rudge wrote to a journal to complain that he had not been identified as the inventor and maker of the apparatus at one of Friese Greene's fulsomely reported demonstrations, the overlooked inventor could say plainly that "I have been perfecting this invention for the last fifteen years" and "I have exhibited it publicly for two years" (Coe 1962, 93) without raising any follow-up interest from the editor. It was Friese Greene who was in the center of things to the profession and who got all the attention. Thomas Bolas, the editor of *The Photographic Review*, commented that "Mr. Greene promises us as wide a departure from the old lines of photography as Mr. Muybridge when he showed us the horse and other animals on the screen" (October 19, 1889, 189).

Friese Greene never actually provided the wide departure he so often promised, but two other American inventors, both intriguing subjects for further research, created double-system apparatus derived from dissolving magic lantern practice in the next years. The first was Robert Dempsey Gray, a lens maker at a shop on Beekman Street in New York City, who in the spring of 1895 developed a unique double-image camera and projector that he patented in both America and Germany (Gray 1895, 1895a). Gray's two patents describe an apparatus using the same fundamental approach to moving pictures, but have important practical differences. Gray's approach was to make a single-lens device, with a rotating disk set at a 45⁰ angle behind the lens. Half of this disk was mirrored, so that as it rotated it directed the image to be recorded to two different locations at right angles to each other on a band of film as it moved around the inside of the machine. Intermittent movement was provided by a double claw engaging perforations on the film, and the synchronization of the entire apparatus was established by linking all moving parts to a master gear turned by a crank. In projection, two lamphouses at right angles to each other were placed at the appropriate aperture where the image had been recorded, with the revolving half-mirrored disk now recombining the alternately spaced images before the single lens.

Gray, who is hardly mentioned in any history of the invention of moving pictures, would simply remain the author of another suggested apparatus (albeit one drawn from dissolving magic lantern practice) were it not for the significant differences in his two patents, whose applications were filed only eleven weeks apart. The American application was filed first, on March 9, 1895. Here, Gray uses a single band of quite wide film that moves fully across two adjoining sides of the interior of his machine, and at the same time undulates from a higher position along the back (opposite the lens) to a lower position along the side (parallel to the lens). The rotating half-mirrored disk places alternate images not only on the back and on the side as the film moves, but also on the lower half of the film at the back and on the upper half of the film at the side. Just eleven weeks later, in his German application of June 2, 1895, and still using the same basic layout and mechanical principles, Gray has changed his apparatus into one using two separate bands of narrower film, with separate feed and take-up reels, and two separate intermittent claw mechanisms instead of one. The changes in Gray's apparatus are all practical. In those eleven weeks (less whatever time it took to get an application to Germany and arrange its filing), Gray reduced the considerable strain on the long film band by substituting double bands moving a shorter distance, improved the registration of the images by dispensing with the undulation of the single band, and secured the focus and tension of the film at the moment of exposure (or projection) by adding pressure rollers and a tensioning spring to keep each of the two bands flat and precisely positioned.

The changes in the German patent could have been made only by observing the problems found in a working machine made to the American patent design. The prompt second model machine attests to Gray's skills in identifying and solving the problems of his first machine and to an intense period of development, as does the fact of his application for a patent in Germany, which was both considerably more expensive and more difficult to achieve than a patent in the United States—or in Great Britain. So here we have another pioneer, with a working apparatus quickly improved. And there the story ends, for nothing else is yet known of Gray or his work, perhaps unresearched since his design would not have been a potential precedent for any of the extensive later American patent lawsuits between Edison, Biograph, Armat, Jenkins, and other inventors and man-

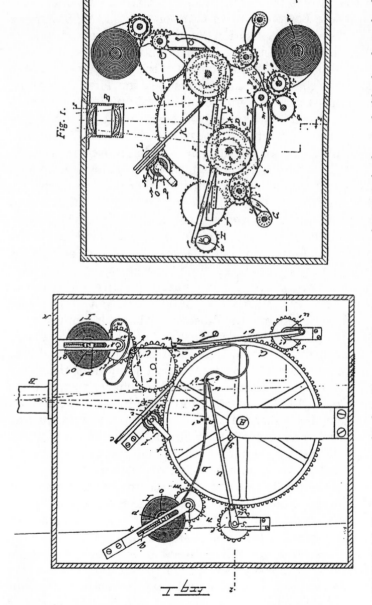

FIGURE 16. Two versions of Robert Dempsey Gray's apparatus of 1895. Left, the single film band, single claw intermittent version from his American patent of March 9, and right, the double film band, double claw intermittent apparatus from his German patent of June 2.

ufacturers that have been the basic record for American historians of the period.

A somewhat similar fate befell the lantern-style apparatus of Owen A. Eames of Boston, who presented his machine to a meeting of the Boston Camera Club on April 1, 1895, just six days after his patent application (Eames 1895). After several years of work on instantaneous photography and "the construction of various devices for use in that branch of the art," Eames came to the conclusion that "three things must be done. First, there must be a constant passage of light; second, the film must travel continuously; and third, the speed of the film must be reduced by using more than one lens" (Eames 1896, 330). The Eames Animatoscope used two reciprocating lenses that moved at the same speed as a film band wide enough to take side-by-side images from each lens. A disk shutter ensured that only one lens at a time was either recording or projecting, and yet provided a continuous bright image on the screen, as with dissolving magic lantern slides. Nine published frames of film are evidence of the machine's workability, but nothing is yet known of any public use of the apparatus. Of all the double-image systems that were inferred from dissolving magic lantern practice only one is known to have had successful public exhibition at the very beginnings of the cinema, the Bioscop of Max Skladanowsky.

Born April 30, 1863, in Berlin, Max Skladanowsky was apprenticed in photography, then glass painting, and finally in optics with the firm of Hagedorn, manufacturers of theatrical lighting and magic lanterns (the most extensive treatment is Castan 1995). In 1879 he went on tour with his father, Carl, and older brother Emil (born 1859), presenting dissolving magic lantern shows, and from 1881 through 1890 the family presented magic lantern, water fountain, and mechanical theater shows throughout Germany and Central Europe. At one point for an elaborate varieté tour Max built a complex nine-projector dissolving magic lantern rig; in 1890 he and Emil constructed a mobile mechanical theater with which they toured Germany in 1891 and Budapest, Vienna, and Scandinavia in 1892.

With the beginnings of his interest in moving pictures, the facts of Max Skladanowsky's work become ever more obscure. He did not help his own claim to be "the first inventor of the cinema" by his later continual changing of his story and ever-earlier dating of his experiments, or by substituting his later single-lens Bioscop II projector for his original double-lens apparatus in several museum exhibitions in the 1920s and 1930s. Skladanowsky was also not helped by an intensive campaign to discredit his work orchestrated by Oskar Messter, even in the face of Messter's own commissioned studies (Castan 1995, 174–76). Messter was quite properly nicknamed "the founder of the German film industry," but he also wanted to be the very first of his country's film pioneers. As if this were not enough for a moderately successful lanternist and varieté performer to contend with, Skladanowsky's reputation was also battered by its appropriation for political purposes, first by the National Socialists in the 1930s and then again by the German Democratic Republic after 1945, since his Berlin residence, workshops, and test exhibition sites happened to fall in the eastern zone of the divided country.

Skladanowsky built a camera for 54 mm film that was probably ready in early 1894, and not in the often-cited summer of 1892. The film ran at about ten frames per second from a lower feed reel to an upper take-up reel, with the intermittent movement provided by a worm gear. A test film of brother Emil cavorting on the roof of the building at Schönhauser Allee 146 in Berlin proved the capability of the machine, and was later turned into a flip book. Knowing that he had a workable camera, Skladanowsky turned to solving the issues involved in making a projector, which was ready sometime in the summer of 1895. His Bioscop was nearly as tall as a grown man, and like all of Skladanowsky's apparatus (most of which survives in either the Bundesarchiv in Berlin or the Filmmuseum in Potsdam) was hardly an example of fine mechanical craftsmanship, but rather the robust and practical construction of an inveterate tinkerer and travelling showman who needed the security that nothing would break down on the road. As a consequence the Bioscop had heavy wooden carpentry and not fine cabinetmaking, and was equipped with heavy gears that could drive a train. The substantial worm gear intermittent drove two loops of 54 mm film with metal eyelets reinforcing their perforations. A half-circle disk shutter in front of the lens, with deeply incised jagged teeth directly taken from early magic lantern dissolvers, blended the images of the two lenses on the screen, providing an almost flickerless presentation.

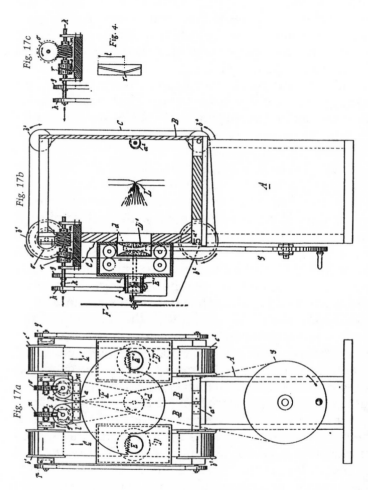

114

FIGURE 17. The Bioscop double-band projector of Max Skladanowsky, 1895. The worm-gear intermittent movment is seen in fig. 17c, and at the top left of fig. 17b. The apparatus was driven by a hand crank at the lower front of the machine.

Tested in the main room of the Sello public house in the Berlin suburb of Pankow in July 1895, the Skladanowsky projector was booked to open at the Wintergarten Theatre on November 1, 1895, the same date as Max's application for a patent on his intermittent movement (Skladanowsky 1895), and on that date he initiated the first public screenings of moving pictures for a paying audience in Europe. The Bioscop was exhibited on the 'Small Stage' (Kleine Bühne) at the Wintergarten, about 250 feet from the main stage, an eight-month-old addition to the Wintergarten premises that was intended for smaller, self-contained acts. It also had the advantage that the screen could be seen only by those seated directly in front of it, since the architecture of the Wintergarten kept this part of the theater somewhat isolated from the audiences at the main stage and in the open circulating spaces. As one of the leading varieté theaters in Europe, renowned for breaking new acts, the Wintergarten drew a sophisticated middle- and upper-middle-class audience, which freely circulated through its spaces and kept up a lively exchange during their evening out.

Installed in mid-October to test the apparatus and the rigging of the stage, the Bioscop was placed behind the downstage screen, which was kept wet to enhance its transparency. The opening program on November 1 included the films *Italienischer Bauerntanz* (an Italian peasant dance), *Komisches Reck* (the Brothers Milton, dressed as man and wife, in a comic tumbling act), *Der Jongleur* (Paul Petras in a traditional juggling act), *Das boxende Känguruh* (the animal trainer Mr. Delaware and his boxing kangaroo), *Akrobatisches Potpourri* (the seven members of the Family Grunato in a gymnastic act), *Kamarinskija* (the Three Tscherpanofs essaying a Russian national dance, in costume), *Ringkampf zwischen Greiner und Sandow* (a wrestling match between Ringer and Eugene Sandow), and *Apotheose*, also called *Der Erfinder des Bioscops* (Max and younger brother Eugen Skladanowsky bow a finale to the audience). Also announced for the opening program was the film *Serpentintanz*, starring Mlle. Ançion, but no press reports of the November showings mention this film and it is doubtful that it was shown during this engagement at the Wintergarten.

Given good pre-opening publicity by the Wintergarten, the Berlin press assembled on Friday evening November 1, and was

enthusiastic about the new presentation. The Bioscop was compared to the work of Ottomar Anschütz, and clearly was the hit
of the new three and one-half hour varieté program. *Der Artist*
wrote that "with the Bioscop the Skladanowskys have invented
something magnificent: artists appear magically on the stage in
this act, life-sized and comparable to the electrical Schnellseher,
so that one is astounded. The presentation is undoubtedly the
most amusing of the evening, and it is sad that it comes at the
end of the program." For the *Berliner Tageblatt* the new act was
a "most enjoyable shadow play" and to the *Volks-Zeitung* the
Bioscop was "indisputably the most interesting presentation, an
Edison Kinetoscope made life-size, which reproduces the movements of dancers, tumblers, and wrestlers with meticulous precision." The *Staatsbürger-Zeitung* was also clearly astonished,
commenting "How he does it only the Devil knows." Audiences
at the Wintergarten that Friday night shared the excitement of
the press, with the *Kleine Journal* noting "Applause and flowers
are the coinage with which the public at the Wintergarten
acknowledges their thanks. On Friday the applause would not
end, and the flower sellers on Unter den Linden must have done
a hearty business" (Castan 1995, 60).

With this exhibition at the Wintergarten Theatre, Max
Skladanowsky conceived his Bioscop as the latest in a long line
of mechanical varieté acts with which he and his brothers had
been associated, and during the course of November his presentation of living pictures was contracted by two of the leading
showplaces of Europe: the Folies Bergère in Paris and the Empire
Theatre in London's Leicester Square. Before leaving for Paris,
Max and Emil Skladanowsky presented their film program again
at the Concerthaus in Hamburg during the period of December
15–25. At the end of the month they went to Paris, and installed
the Bioscop at the Folies Bergère, ready to open as advertised on
January 1, 1896. What happened next is shrouded in mystery and
has been a subject of controversy for many years. But it is clear
that in Paris the brothers ran into competition for the first time,
as the Lumière Cinématographe opened to the public on the
boulevard du Capucines on December 28. The Skladanowskys
and the director of the Folies apparently saw the Lumière apparatus on the next day, and in Emil's recollection were "astounded
and surprised" at what they saw: "The pictures were steadier,

sharper and longer than our own" (Castan 1995, 77). Following this screening, the management of the Folies cancelled the Skladanowsky presentation, citing patent difficulties with their apparatus. The brothers were paid off and left the city.

Did they go on to London to fulfil their contract at the Empire Theatre? None of the later Skladanowsky reminiscences, partial autobiographies, and journalistic interviews mentions the London engagement, although most of their writings were generated in a tumultous three-way fight between Skladanowsky, the Lumière brothers, and Messter that by the 1930s had turned heavily nationalistic. A printed poster for the Bioscop dating from 1896 advertises both the Paris and London showings, as well as one in Blackpool (Zglinicki 1979, 245). But one recently unearthed account suggests that they may have travelled on to London, although without much public success. In a letter to *To-Day's Cinema*, F. A. Pickering gives an eyewitness account of the Skladanowsky's appearance at the Wintergarten in Berlin: "the pictures were projected from the back and were shown on a small stage at the end of the building. . . . Five or six very short pictures were shown. . . . The pictures were small in size, very shaky but distinct." Pickering, who was an agent for the Empire Theatre in London was "on one of my periodical tours of the Continent in search of suitable attractions" and "had already read of the moving picture apparatus and was most anxious to see one." He immediately arranged for the Bioscop to appear at the Empire, and the contract was concluded by his directors, which undoubtedly led to the printed German program citing London as one of the Skladanowsky venues. Shortly after visiting Berlin, Pickering left on a trip to Arabia and when he returned, he found the Lumière Cinématographe installed at the Empire Theatre. Pickering recalled, "I asked my chief (Dundas Slater) what had happened to the Bioscop I had booked, and he explained to me that the pictures being so small and the items so short, the audience took very little interest in them therefore the directors decided to remove the Bioscop from the stage and show it in a structure in the foyer and charged 1 S. entrance; but it still failed to attract, and the engagement was concluded" (Pickering 1936).

No confirming evidence for Pickering's vividly detailed and seemingly reliable statement has yet been found in the Empire program booklets and the London appearance of the Bioscop remains questionable. But until 1996 it was not even a question for further research; the episode illustrates with particular clarity the urgent atmosphere surrounding moving pictures at the end of 1895. "I had already read of the moving picture apparatus and was most anxious to see one," says Pickering, and from the secrecy that surrounded the Skladanowsky apparatus before its premiere at the Wintergarten, he could not have read about their Bioscop. That the Skladanowsky machine made its public debut at one of Europe's most important variety theaters, and was quickly booked at two others in major capital cities is a reminder of how quickly news of any moving picture apparatus was spread internationally. Both the Anschütz Schnellseher and the Edison Kinetoscope peep-show viewers were quickly exhibited in many countries around the world, and projected moving pictures were also an international phenomenon from the very beginning. That this is in part because inventors defined the problem of moving pictures on the screen as the next logical step beyond elaborate magic lantern dissolving slide sets and mechanical slides is clear, just as each alternative invention of the chronophotographers or the appearance of the Edison Kinetoscope brought forth new issues in creating living pictures that spurred inventors and showmen on to new solutions.

The Kinetoscope was a very influential apparatus on this international community of inventors and tinkerers. As soon as it appeared, the almost universal reaction was "Make it project." Edison himself talked of this from the beginning, but did nothing about it and when the initial sales of Dickson's apparatus were brisk, he fully abandoned any attempts at screen projection, famously prophesying that if a screen projection machine existed, only three would be needed to service the entire United States. His most conservative approach to the entertainment business, which he never understood, and his misunderstanding of the significance of the apparatus that had emerged from his own laboratory, gave him short-term profits and long-term acclaim as the inventor of movies.

Many others saw the situation quite differently. Already in late December 1894, John Anderton of Birmingham, England, and Alfred Lomax of Blackpool applied for a patent that allowed the Edison Kinetoscope to be viewed by more than one person at a time by rigging one or more prisms above its viewing eyepiece (Anderton and Lomax 1894). Just six days later in early January 1895, Cecil Wray, an electrical engineer in Bradford, England, applied for his patent on a somewhat less practical accessory including a prism and a combination of lenses that would turn the Kinetoscope into a projection apparatus (Wray 1895). In November 1895, Henri Joly, a former gymnastics instructor at Joinville, where Marey occasionally took chronophotographs, patented his Photozootrope, a kinetoscope that could be viewed by four people simultaneously and ran two different film bands at once (Joly 1895). Others also worked on alternatives to the Kinetoscope, like C. Francis Jenkins and the group led by Herman Casler in America. Some initially reproduced Edison's machine, like Robert Paul in England. But most of those inspired by the Kinetoscope and its band of flexible celluloid film simply began straightaway to work on projection apparatus. Among them were Thomas Armat and the Latham family in the United States, and the brothers August and Louis Lumière in France.

Born in 1867 and raised on a farm near Richmond, Indiana, C. Francis Jenkins saw his future as a professional inventor: he was just of the generation to have been inspired by the successful lives of Thomas Edison, Cyrus McCormick, and the other inventor/builders of late-nineteenth-century America. Jenkins always looked to the future—he would spend most of his time in the 1920s working on television systems, and by the end of his career held over 400 patents ranging from automobiles to aviation. From humble beginnings, he devoted his spare time from work as a civil service stenographer in Washington, D.C., to self-improvement and invention. He apparently began searching for a method for "the recording and reproduction of action" in 1891 or 1892, by the following year employing a mechanic with funding from James P. Freeman. It was during this time that he may have worked with a rotary-lens chronophotographic camera: the records are very confused as a result of conflicting and inaccurate testimony both at many later patent trials and at formal reviews of his work during his lifetime. It is certain that the appearance of the Edison Kinetoscope changed the course of his work, and by November 1894 he was able to apply for a patent on a kinetoscope viewer using perforated celluloid film that just avoided Edison's prior work (Jenkins 1894). He called his viewer the Phantoscope, as he did all of his early apparatus, which lent further confusion in many later accounts of his career. This first Jenkins Phantoscope was displayed at the Pure Food Exposition in Washington, D.C., in November 1894, but it is not known if it was operated and it disappeared quickly from sight. By December, Jenkins applied for a second patent for a combination motion picture camera and projector that featured continuously moving film three inches wide and a wheel of four rotating lenses (Jenkins 1894a). Certainly Jenkins was in no financial condition to begin manufacturing his apparatus, and since he had just met a like-minded student at the Bliss School of Electricity, Thomas Armat, the two began discussing how the moving picture machine could be exploited (the most thorough review of the partnership's work and warfare is Gosser 1988).

Thomas Armat brought financial substance to the partnership the two men agreed to in March 1895. A former railroad bookeeper and part-time inventor who had already received patents for electrical railway apparatus, Armat had been impressed by seeing the Anschütz electrical Schnellseher at the Columbian Exposition in Chicago in 1893, and later by Edison's Kinetoscope; he initially found Jenkins an equally committed partner. The two quickly discovered that Jenkins's system of continuously moving film was impractical, and by August had developed another machine, this one using a heavy intermittent formed by gears ordered from Boston (Jenkins and Armat 1895). This was a kind of expanded Maltese Cross gear with fourteen slots that was extremely similar in design and precisely the same in function as the thirteen-sided gear used in Anschütz's last machine, his Projecting Electrotachyscope of November 1894. Although an improvement, the great strain this gearing placed on the celluloid film (along with its noise) caused the pair to abandon their "Boston gear" after only a few weeks, and substitute another intermittent design, patterned after the beater movement described by Georges Demenÿ in December 1893. This further improved the Jenkins-Armat machine, and the partners hastily made plans for its public debut at the Cotton States Exhibition in Atlanta, Georgia, opening in September 1895.

The developmental history of the Phantoscope is unique in the story of the invention of moving pictures. No other inventor, or partnership, went so rapidly through so many different concepts of how their machine should operate, with such clearly identifiable precedents, as did Jenkins and Armat. Four different types of operation were used in only a few months: the continuous-run apparatus derived from the Kinetoscope, an unknown "gradual acceleration" machine, the Boston gear apparatus derived from Anschütz, and the beater apparatus similar to Demenÿ's. It is overwhelmingly more common for an inventor to have taken an approach to solving the riddle of moving pictures and then stuck with it, whether derived from other practice or not, sometimes for several years after it was surpassed by the work of others. Even Edison, who tried several concepts for the Kinetoscope, and was clearly influenced at various stages by his own prior work and that of Anschütz and Marey, took several years to pass through these developmental stages. Perhaps Jenkins and Armat were more assiduous in their search for moving pictures than Edison, even with resources and international contacts that were miniscule in comparison with Edison's "invention factory" in West Orange. Perhaps Jenkins and Armat had a striking ability to conceptualize their work from a variety of perspectives—although there is no evidence of this in their later, separate, careers. After this initial period of development, and through the turn of the century, neither man made any significant or radical contributions to the improvement of moving picture technology. If anything, the reverse is true: Jenkins held on to some of his early Phantoscope apparatus for several years, claiming unknown "improvements"; and Armat, in his later patented refinements to their joint machine (Armat 1896) includes as an afterthought a rather silly alternative intermittent that lends him no credibility as a mechanical innovator.

So what was this team up to during this period of intense concentration on developing motion picture apparatus? They worked on nothing else, they had no fully established laboratory or machine shop, ordering parts as needed from as far away as Boston. Apparently, as they left for Atlanta with their latest Phantoscope, they left the construction of two additional machines to Armat's younger brother Hunter Armat (Gosser 1988, 2). From what is known of the two ambitious young Washingtonians, and from their existing apparatus, they seem not to have been established within any fine mechanical or optical tra-

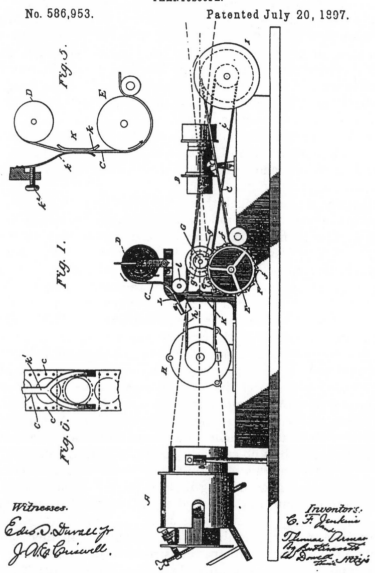

(No Model.)   2 Sheets—Sheet 1.

C. F. JENKINS & T. ARMAT.
PHANTOSCOPE.

No. 586,953.   Patented July 20, 1897.

Witnesses.   *Inventors.*

FIGURE 18. The Phantoscope of Charles Francis Jenkins and Thomas Armat, from their patent applied for on August 28, 1895, and issued July 20, 1897, showing its large "Boston gear" intermittent, center.

ditions: they aspired to be professional inventors in the grand American tradition of tinkerers. Intelligent and resourceful, they both nonetheless had patent experience, and easy access to the full records of the main U.S. Patent Office, located in their adopted home city. It is likely that the rapid development of the Phantoscope was simply a process of building and rebuilding their intermittent to all options that they could find until the operation of the machine settled into its best form; there seems to have been little basic research underlying the apparatus.

With the exhibition of the Phantoscope in Atlanta, the relationship between the partners began to break up. Since they had no working camera, Jenkins and Armat exhibited Edison Kinetoscope films, supplied by a friend at the Columbia Phonograph Company, the Edison franchisee in Washington. Charging twenty-five cents admission, the Phantoscope was installed in a double-theater arrangement using two of the three machines with the third in reserve in case of breakdown. One audience would watch the show while the other side of their concession was emptied and then refilled for the next show; Jenkins and Armat spent long hours each night repairing torn sprockets and ripped film (Gosser 1988, 2). On October 13, 1895, Jenkins left Atlanta with one of the projectors and went to his brother's wedding in Richmond, Indiana, giving an exhibition there. He had promised to return to Atlanta, with the machine, but never did. In the meantime, fire struck the end of the midway where the Phantoscope was exhibited, destroying several exhibits and damaging one of the projectors. Armat returned to Washington and began to make more improvements on the Phantoscope, and Jenkins now decided to claim sole authorship of the apparatus, launching a bitter feud with Armat that would prevail until the deaths of both men—and beyond into the literature of film history.

While Jenkins and Armat were busy developing their various Phantoscopes, another Kinetoscope-inspired team began to work on screen projection: Gray and Otway Latham. In August 1894, the brothers opened a Kinetoscope parlor at 83 Nassau Street in New York City to exhibit the filmed record of a six-round boxing match between Michael Leonard and Jack Cushing, which they had produced at the Black Maria the previous June. Bringing their father, Woodville Latham, and a college friend, Enoch J. Rector, into their newly formed Kinetoscope Exhibition Company, the brothers were primarily interested in fight films, seeing an opportunity to capitalize on the popularity of a sport that was at the time banned in most states across America. The group may have suggested that Edison and Dickson enlarge the capacity of the Kinetoscope (to 150 feet) and lower its running speed (to thirty frames per second) in order to accommodate full one-minute boxing rounds. In any case, it was with six enlarged-capacity Kinetoscopes that the group exhibited their first boxing films in August 1894. By September, they had a second fight film ready, between the heavyweight champion James Corbett and Peter Cushing. But by September, the team was already at work on screen projection.

When the Lathams formed the Lambda Company to develop new film apparatus, their technical expertise came from Eugene Lauste, a former Edison employee and reputedly a brilliantly capable machinist, and from W. K. L. Dickson, still employed by Edison but lending surreptitious advice to the new concern. Dickson supplied an old Kinetoscope and prints of films while visiting the Lambda workshops weekly to lend his advice, and a projector called the Eidoloscope was tested at the Lathams's shop by December 1894. This was at first a 35 mm machine with continuously running film, like the Kinetoscope, but was quickly enlarged into an apparatus using two-inch-wide film bands to allow a brighter image on the screen. The Lathams also developed a motion picture camera to supply films, which was ready by the end of February; attempts to use the camera as a projector (with an intermittent movement) proved difficult, as the standard problems of tearing sprocket holes and excessive wear on the film appeared, caused in part by the shrinkage of the celluloid during development, which meant the wide band no longer properly fit the sprockets of the apparatus. This convinced the group that their continuous-movement Eidoloscope projector derived from Kinetoscope practice was the preferred machine: as Woodville Latham later testified, "the life of a film used in a machine where the film is moved continuously is greatly longer than in a machine where the movement is intermittent" (Musser 1990, 94).

On the afternoon of April 21. 1895, the Lathams gave a demonstration of their system to the press, projecting a short film made on clear Eastman stock to journalists at their Frankfort Street premises. "The pictures shown yesterday portrayed the antics of some boys at play. . . . They wrestled, jumped, fought, and tumbled over one another. Near where the boys were romping a man sat reading a paper and smoking a pipe. Even the puffs of smoke could be plainly seen, as could also a man's movements when he took a handkerchief from his pocket" wrote the *New York Sun* reporter, who also mischievously called Thomas Edison to get his reaction to the new device. Edison's first response, characteristically, was to belittle the Latham accomplishment, which was the first public projection of moving pictures on celluloid in the United States, and to flatly state that the Latham machine was "a kinetoscope" and that "the throwing of the pictures on a screen was the very first thing I did with the kinetoscope. I didn't think much of that, because the pictures were crude, and there seemed to me to be no commercial value in that feature of the machine." Edison's concluding remarks staked his claim to any kind of moving picture device: "If they carry the machine around the country, calling it by some other name, that's a fraud, and I shall prosecute whoever does it. I've applied for patents long ago" (*New York Sun*, April 22, 1895, 2).

One element of the Latham device had not been patented by Edison, and would later play a crucial part in the ongoing patent wars that prominently shaped the development of the American film industry: the so-called Latham Loop. Because they were primarily interested in boxing films consisting of several rounds of action, the Latham camera needed to be able to use long lengths of film in a single reel. Their first film intended for commercial exhibition was a boxing match between Young Griffo (Albert Griffiths) and Charles Barnett taken on May 4 and photographed in eight minutes of continuous action, comprising four 90-second rounds of fighting with a half-minute rest period in between. The Latham camera ran continuously during the bout. Directly pulling this length of film through the camera, with its greater weight and mechanical inertia, caused the sprocket holes to be repeatedly torn, a problem not so prominent in machines using shorter lengths of film. The Latham camera therefore provided top and bottom drive sprockets on either side of the camera aperture, with a loop of film between the upper sprocket and the intermittent sprocket to isolate the intermittent motion at the aperture from the inertia and strain of the feed mechanism, a feature probably designed by Dickson or Lauste, although all the Lambda participants later claimed the innovation as their own. This loop was retained in the Latham projector with its continuously moving film, again to relieve the strain on the film due to the weight and inertia of the long lengths stored on the feed and take-up reels, which had primitive friction adjustments to keep the film tensioned as it ran through the apparatus (Latham 1896, 1896a).

Unusually, the Lathams patented their apparatus well after it had been developed and put to use, with legal protections first applied for in Great Britain (March 3) and France (March 31) and then in America (June 1). This strange pattern may have been a reaction to Edison's threats at the moment of their first press showing of the Eidoloscope, with the Lathams initially establishing foreign protection (there is no indication of any use of the apparatus in Europe) as an extra support to their subsequent American application, and as a test of how Edison might react to the establishment of their machine as a legally protected competitor. Whatever the reason, it is certainly the case that most inventors sought patent protection as soon as a viable machine was either finished or near completion, and before any public use or sale. Some, like Edison himself, even patented before the "final" version of their apparatus was ready, making physical modifications to the machinery after the design specifications were submitted.

Certainly the Eidoloscope was in public use on May 20, 1895, when the Lathams opened a storefront theater at 156 Broadway in New York City to show their boxing match between Griffo and Barnett, after a few weeks moving downtown to another storefront on Park Row, the center of the newspaper industry. In late August, they opened at the Olympic vaudeville theater in Chicago, and by September were at the Cotton States Exposition in Atlanta, where the Jenkins and Armat Phantoscope was on exhibit, as well as the Edison Kinetoscope. Lambda seems to have made about a half-dozen machines in all, and sold the apparatus to an otherwise unidentified exibitor named Vandergrift, who used the apparatus in Philadelphia, and to D. C. Porter, who exhibited in Rochester and Syracuse. The home territory of

Virginia was covered by a nephew, LeRoy Latham, who used the apparatus in Norfolk (Musser 1990, 99–100). They supplied films of their boxing matches, and also photographed wrestling matches, Niagara Falls, dancing girls, and a horse race taken at Sheepshead Bay on Long Island.

Despite their early entry into screen projection, and the sale and dissemination of their apparatus across the Eastern half of the United States, the Eidoloscope did not become established as a breakthrough apparatus. A mechanical system with continuously moving film was not an adequate technological solution to projection, although the Eidoloscope achieved some positive press reports, including one that contended that "You'll see people and things as they are. If they wink their other eye, even though not so expressively as Miss Cissy Fitzgerald winks hers, or Thomas C. Platt winks his, you will see the lid on its way down and up. If their hair raises in fright, or grows gray in a half hour, you'll see all the details of the change" (*New York World*, May 28, 1895, p. 30). Although the Jenkins and Armat Phantoscope would be rescued by circumstances in early 1896, no such intervention was in the offing for the Eidoloscope, no matter that the Lathams had presented the first commercially projected motion pictures for a paying audience in the United States. It would be yet another apparatus inspired by the Kinetoscope that startled the entertainment world at the end of 1895, this one the creation of two brothers in Lyon, Auguste and Louis Lumière.

Almost the only incontrovertable statement about the origins of the Lumière apparatus, the Cinématographe, is that work on the machine was begun as a result of the appearance of the Edison Kinetoscope. Amidst a vast literature on these important pioneers, there is not yet an adequate historical study of the development, dissemination, and ultimate dissolution of the Lumière motion picture interests, which were so prominent at the beginnings of the cinema but at a standstill by 1898 and finished in 1901. The Lumière story has long been caught in a maelstrom of scholarly contention over possession of the title "the true inventor of moving pictures" that pits supporters of Étienne-Jules Marey against those of the Lumières, supporters of the Lumières against Edison (and all others), and that finds the Lumière camp today trying to fend off insurgent new research that gives precedence to the work of Georges Demenÿ. As a result, much needed work on the Lumière brothers is yet to be done. Generally reliable older sources (Sadoul 1946, 1964; Bessy and Duca 1948) have been superceded in important respects by new information, yet some of the most widely known recent publications (Chardère 1985, 1987, 1995; Rittaud-Hutinet 1985, 1990, 1995, 1995a) need to be used with great circumspection.

By the mid-1890s, the Lumière family firm was one of the most important suppliers of photographic film and supplies in Europe. Founded in 1880 in the Montplaisir quarter of Lyon, the Société A. Lumière et fils had only modest success until August and Louis returned from their military service and developed apparatus that mechanized production of the company's gelatin-bromide plates. Louis then formulated the emulsion of an outstanding photographic plate, the famous "étiquette bleue," and by 1895 the company was making some 1.3 million étiquette bleue plates annually, plus 50,000 plates of other sorts and over 12,000 feet of photographic paper (Sadoul 1946, 185). The two brothers already had some fifteen patents, mostly for various photographic processes and machinery, including their first attempts at a synthetic color process.

The most plausible of several stories about the origins of the Lumière work on moving pictures comes from the factory's chief mechanic, Charles Moisson, who wrote in 1930 that the father, Antoine Lumière, came into his office on day in the summer of 1894 while he was talking with Louis and took a piece of the Kinetoscope film *Barbershop Scene* out of his pocket, saying to Louis, "This is what you have to make, because Edison sells this at insane prices and the agents are trying to make films here in France so they can get them cheaper." Other sources suggest that it was Antoine's friend, the Parisian photographer Clément-Maurice, who obtained a piece of film from the Werner brothers' Kinetoscope parlor on the boulevard Poissonnière. And later, Auguste Lumière claimed that he had come up with the film after seeing the Kinetoscope in the rue de la République in Lyon. Whatever the case, as Louis and Auguste began to work on moving pictures, they chose precisely the same size of celluloid film as used in the Kinetoscope, about 1½ inches, or 35mm, wide. Their research was in full swing by the end of the year.

Precisely what development process their apparatus went through in Lyon is shrouded in mystery. The brothers obtained supplies of celluloid film from the European Blair Camera Company, and began almost immediately to seek their own film manufacturing capability with Victor Planchon (see chapter 4). It is clear that in addition to the Kinetoscope they knew the work and apparatus of Étienne-Jules Marey and Georges Demenÿ, with the latter showing them plans for his "great projector" and its claw intermittent movement. The legend that they found the solution to projection in a single sleepless night when Louis remembered the foot-pedal works of a sewing machine, is hardly credible. Yet development there was, and recent reexamination of the existing Lumière negatives by staff at the Centre nationale de la cinématographie has revealed through the examination of frame lines and image placement on the negatives that there were three early machines, not the previously known two.

The apparatus that emerged from the Lumière workshops under the guidance of Charles Moisson was an elegant, lightweight, and sophisticated piece of mechanical design, patented in France on February 13, 1895, and ultimately named the Cinématographe (Lumière 1895). Just 13 inches high (including the upper film holder), 5 inches deep, and 7½ inches wide, the Cinématographe was enclosed in a wooden case and turned by a hand crank. Intermittent movement was provided by a double-claw movement pulling on the single circular perforation at either side of each frame; the movement of the claw was originally determined by the off-center mounting of one end on a circular disk, but this arrangement was quickly modified in an addition to their basic patent on March 30 into an ingenious triangular cam rotating inside a squared frame (Lumiere 1895a). A two-bladed shutter ran behind the lens, and the apparatus had neither sprockets nor rollers, a pair of leaf springs tensioning the film at the aperture. When used as a camera a small wooden light-tight box holding 50 feet of film was mounted at the top of the machine. For projection, the film was hung from an open rack replacing the film box, the rear of the machine was opened, and it was mounted in front of a lantern. This was normally a Molteni lantern, later supplied with a spherical water-filled condenser to reduce the heat on the film. The Cinématographe could also be used as a printer by threading a negative and unexposed positive through the machine simultaneously and allowing light to expose the raw stock through the lens aperture in the front of the machine. Weighing just fourteen pounds, this was an easily portable, smooth running, relatively quiet machine whose main drawback was a serious flicker when run at almost any speed, due to the design of the shutter and the amount of time it took the claw movement to pull down the next frame of film. The flicker was a small price to pay for a portable and reliable machine with many superior features.

The Cinématographe made its debut at the Société d'encouragement pour l'industrie nationale in Paris on March 22, 1895, where it was called a "kinetoscope de projection." One film was

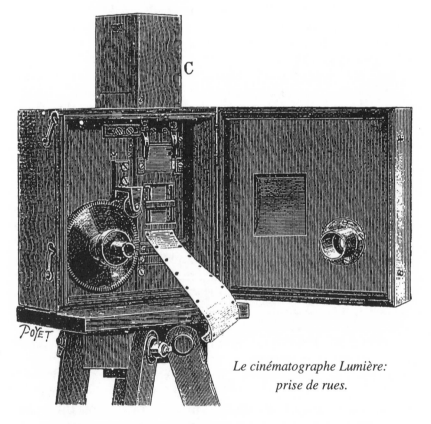

Le cinématographe Lumière:
prise de rues.

FIGURE 19. The Lumière Cinématographe set up for use as a camera, from an 1896 engraving. The light-tight box C held the unexposed negative film, which simply rerolled inside the camera when the door was shut.

shown, and the presentation was just one part of a program devoted to a discussion of the Lumière photographic plates and their work on color photographic processes. A number of other professional demonstrations followed, at the Sorbonne on April 17, at a photographic congress in Lyon on June 10, at the Revue générale des sciences pures et appliquées in Paris on July 11, for family and friends at Antoine Lumière's home in La Ciotat on September 21, for the Belgian photographer's association on November 10, again in Brussels for the Literary and Artistic Circle two days later, in Louvain on November 13, and at the opening of the Faculté des sciences at the Louvre again on November 16. While these early demonstrations of the Cinématographe were under way, Louis Lumière arranged for the scientific instrument maker Jules Carpentier in Paris to make an initial group of twenty-five machines. Carpentier, who had bought the workshop of the physicist Heinrich Daniel Rühmkorff, the inventor of the electrical coil used in the Anschütz Schnellseher, was a manufacturer of electrical machines, small cameras, precision instruments, and electrical apparatus. In 1895 he was also working on his own double-system moving picture machine, but nonetheless took up the contract to make the Lumière Cinématographe. Several details were still to be refined: adjustments to the shutter, the precise design of a pressure plate that would secure but not damage the film in the gate, experiments with materials to be used for various parts of the apparatus (see Rittaud-Hutinet 1995, 35–39, 41–43, 50–61, 66, 68–73, 75–79). Meanwhile, other experimenters in France had also turned to working on screen projection.

In early 1895, Henri Joly met a phonograph dealer with a shop in Vincennes, one Charles Pathé, who had been importing the reproduction Edison kinetoscopes made in England by Robert Paul. Pathé installed his machines mostly in fairgrounds and markets, and needed a wider supply of films since the copies wore out quickly and his audiences tired of seeing the same subjects. Pathé gave financial support to Joly in his attempts to make a camera to supply films for his kinetoscopes, and the result was a patented apparatus (Joly 1895a) using the Demenÿ beater movement and 35-mm film that could also be used for screen projection. By autumn, Joly had made the film *Le Bain d'une mondaine* for the Pathé/Paul kinetoscopes with this apparatus. Another early researcher was George William de Bedts, the Paris agent for the European Blair Camera Company, who was in a position to know of most French developments in moving pictures since he supplied celluloid film to most of the active experimenters, including Joly, Lumière, Léon Gaumont, and others. In the second half of 1895 he also began working on a combination camera, projector, and printer called the Kinétographe using a three-toothed mutilated gear intermittent that was nearing completion in November 1895 and early the next year would become the first 35-mm camera patented and offered for sale in France (de Bedts 1896).

All of this activity in the second half of 1895 began to alarm Antoine Lumière, who wrote to his sons from Paris (in a letter unpublished in the Rittaud-Hutinet edited correspondence) that a public showing of the Cinématographe must be arranged quickly, since other apparatus was near completion, and someone else would be first if they did not act. In the end, it was father Antoine with the help of his friend the photographer Clément-Maurice who arranged the first public showing of the Cinématographe at the Salon Indien of the Grand Café at 14 boulevard des Capucines, Paris, on December 28, 1895. The Cinématographe and its Molteni lantern were installed in the cellar room of the café, a ventilated space with its own entrance to the street about 40 feet by 25 feet holding a hundred café chairs. An invited audience saw the Cinématographe in the afternoon, and in the evening thirty-three people paid one Franc each to attend a public screening. The films shown in the first program were *Sortie d'usine, La Voltige, La Pêche aux poissons rouges, Le Débarquement du Congrès de photographie à Lyon, Les Forgerons, Le Jardinier, Le Repas, Le Saut à la couverture, La Place des Cordeliers à Lyon,* and *La Mer.* Each film began with a still image on the screen, before the operator, Charles Moisson, began to turn the crank and the image began to move, causing one wag in the first audience, legendarily Georges Méliès, to shout "It's a magic lantern again!" But, emphatically, this time it was not.

CHAPTER SEVEN

——————— ◙ ———————

Multiple Questions:
The Many Cinemas of 1896–1900

The year 1896, the first full year of moving picture projection, was dominated by three inventor-entrepreneurs, each of whom had a very different approach to the cinema and a different business strategy for its dissemination and exploitation. Their chosen strategies, however—those of the Lumière brothers in France, of Robert William Paul in England, and of Thomas Edison and his associates in America—were only three of many possible approaches to moving picture work and several dozens of "second-generation" figures quickly appeared with their own solutions to moving picture technology and their own alternative ideas about what the cinema could become. At the beginning of 1896, moving pictures existed as either a peep-show experience for individual viewers or as screen projection for groups of spectators. Animated pictures had inherited both technology and repertoire from the world of magic lantern shows and had appeared as a vaudeville or varieté entertainment. But no definitive patterns had been established, and many questions remained unanswered.

Would the new technical marvel become an instrument for instruction? For entertainment? For communication? For news? Would the cinema be a scientific instrument? Would it be seen in the home? Or only by individuals? Would it be the opening, closing, or starring act in theaters? Would it be absorbed into existing entertainments to become simply another piece of technical stagecraft for dramatists? For magicians? For lecturers? Who would make the films? Professionals? Photographers? Amateurs? Would it become a mass experience with the appearance of a "Kodak" for moving pictures that could claim, "You press the button, we do the rest"?

For inventors, showmen, businessmen, entertainers, scientists, visionaries, and the public at large, the remaining years of the nineteenth century and the first years of the twentieth would be devoted to answering these questions. Many answers were tried, and as a result many different cinemas appeared, each requiring its own technological solutions to the reproduction of moving images. Because achieving the first moving pictures already drew on so many existing traditions and experiences, the arena for further exploration and definition of how to implement and exploit the moving image was vast. The proliferation of moving picture technology that arose from this search was in large part a response to the differing needs, demands, and experiences of each proposed definition of the cinema. The primary suggestions that were made for moving pictures in these early days included the cinema as an individual activity that extended the practice of still photography; the cinema as a portable medium of both instruction and amusement that extended the tradition of magic lantern exhibitions; the cinema as an attraction for fixed theaters that involved dramatized or newsworthy presentations; and the cinema as a scientific instrument that opened new and unseen worlds for analysis. In the beginning, moving pictures were not differentiated simply by being fictional creations or recorded documents, by being able to economically replicate stage illusions or by bringing exotic and faraway lands to small-town viewers; for the first generation of its practitioners, moving pictures presented more fundamental questions that determined the kind of technology that they arrayed to achieve a variety of different purposes. The technological frame of moving pictures was a *tabula rasa*, not yet defined as to its content, institutions, or markets. The experiences of the Lumière brothers, Robert Paul, and Thomas Edison would each, in very different ways, influence their contemporaries and begin to define the potential of the cinema.

After their first public screenings in Paris at the end of 1895, the Lumières were approached, most famously by the magician Georges Méliès, by many people who wanted to buy their Cinématographe. In December, they had ordered another two hundred machines from Jules Carpentier, in addition to their first order of twenty-five. With receipts from their Paris showings at the Grand Café reaching an average of 2,500 francs a day by early January 1896, the Lumières decided that their apparatus would at first not be sold publicly. They would reap the profits of their invention, retaining complete control over the machine's use, and the company began to train some of the workers at their factory in Lyon to operate the Cinématographe, for both taking and projecting films. At the same time, the Lumières decided that they would not support the expenses of exploiting their invention with their own capital. Instead, they sold franchises, country by country, to trustworthy agents: each agent would pay a daily fee for the services of the operator, plus his living expenses, while the Cinèmatographe itself and any films would remain the property of the Société A. Lumière et fils.

The franchise for Germany went to a subsidiary of the Stollwerck Company, the Deutsche Automaten Gesellschaft; for Austria and Hungary to Eugène Dupont; for Belgium and the Netherlands to Camille Cerf of the Société de la photographie animée in Brussels; for Switzerland to François-Henri Lavanchy-Clarke; for Russia to Arthur and Ivan Grünewald; for Japan to Inahata Shotaro; for England to Felicien Trewey. The Lumière franchise system seems to have been rather unstructured, relying at times on old friends and business contacts, and at other times on the initiative of the Lumière-employed operators. Trewey in England, for example, was an established showman and friend of Antoine Lumière, while Dupont was a Lyon-born businessman previously engaged in the promotion of French products in Vienna. Stollwerck seems to have made a straightforward business arrangment for the German rights, in line with their previous experience of attempting to promote the Demenÿ Phonoscope, Edison's Kinetoscope, and the moving picture apparatus of Birt Acres. Lavanchy-Clarke in Switzerland, in contrast, seems not to have been subject to the usual contractual arrangements between an agent and the home office in Lyon.

Further, Cinématographe operator Marius Sestier, sent to India and Australia, seems to have himself arranged the local collaboration of Henry Walter Barnett, a Sydney photographer. Whatever the anomalies of the Lumière system (there are too many credible reports of individual sales of the Cinématographe before it was officially available on the market in late February 1897 for them all to be mythical), it was through these franchisees, and sometimes through unattached employees of the Lumière concern in Lyon, that a group of factory-trained operators took the Lumière Cinématographe across six continents during the eighteen months after its debut in Paris. The Cinématographe was notably portable and convertible as a camera, projector, and film printer, so that the Lumière operators had a striking success in conducting pioneering exhibitions as they dispersed around the globe and sent the results of their filmmaking in each location back to Lyon, where selected films entered the Lumière catalogue and could be used by their colleagues in the far-flung Lumière operations. Among the most prominent of these Cinématographe operators who publicized the Lumière firm while closely guarding their machine's technology were Marius Chapuis (Russia), Francis Doublier (Russia, the Netherlands, Germany, India, and China), François-Constant Girel (Germany, Switzerland, France, Japan), Félix Mesguich (France, Russia, Canada, United States), Jean Alexandre Louis Promio (Spain, England, Italy, United States, Egypt, Turkey, Sweden), Marius Sestier (India, Australia), and Gabriel Veyre (Mexico, Cuba, Venezuela, Colombia, Japan, Vietnam) (Aubert and Sequin 1996, 408–417).

The Lumière presentations in most countries followed a similar pattern. First a private screening for opinion-makers or royalty was held, followed by a public opening that was later augmented by the addition of locally made film subjects to the program, a model exemplified by the screenings organized by Eugène Dupont in Vienna. On March 20, 1896, Dupont held a demonstration for an invited audience of dignitaries and scientists at the K. K. Lehr-und Versuchsanstalt für Photographie in Vienna, opening to the public a week later in the mezzanine of the house at Kärntnerstraße 45, with the new "living photography" acclaimed as the sensation of the city within a week. On April 1, a private screening was held at the French Embassy for

FIGURE 20. The Lumière Cinématographe in use as a projector, from an 1896 engraving. The small device on the shelf below the Molteni lantern was used to rewind the films, which fell loosely into a bin below the machine; extra films are on the shelf below the operator.

Kaiser Franz-Joseph I, and before the end of the month Dupont added to his program locally taken views of traffic in front of the Kärtnerstraße and of the central Viennese fire brigade. By the end of the month, he advertised a changing repertoire of new films each week. In July, with two other film shows running in the city, Dupont dropped his original admission price of 50 kreutzer to 30 kreutzer (Bleier-Brody 1960, 27–28).

This archetypal Lumière presentation, repeated in many cities and countries, was intended to achieve maximum publicity and establishment backing for the Cinématographe, yet the apparatus was not for sale and the limited number of travelling operators precluded the establishment of long-term exhibition sites. What did the Lumières intend with this unusal business pattern? The most likely explanation is that they saw the hardware, the Cinématographe, as the vehicle through which they could expand their primary business, the manufacture and sales of photographic film. They pushed forward urgently to develop the manufacturing capacity for celluloid film in parallel with the last stages of work on the Cinématographe (see chapter 4), and the hesitancy of Auguste and Louis Lumière in making their first public exhibition, urged only by father Antoine, may have resulted from the thought that their system was not yet fully ready for public exploitation, since the factory had no regular quality-assured capability of manufacturing celluloid film for the Cinématographe by December 1895.

Such a model would have followed the very successful example of George Eastman and his Kodak system, an example that many others in the photographic supplies business, among them John Henry Blair with his Hawk-Eye roll-film camera, had already tried to emulate with, in 1895, definite signs of success. The Lumière development of the Kinora viewer at the end of 1896, discussed on pages 148–50, reinforces the idea that they saw the potential of moving picture apparatus principally as the means for creating a new market into which their photographic film supply business could expand. The initial excitement as the Cinématographe toured the world, the plaudits received from European nobility and from presidents in the Americas, and the substantial income from public shows through 1897–98 were fickle indicators for the Lumière firm. They held close control of their invention for too long, even knowing that others were close to success in achieving projection, and the burst of activity that appeared within weeks of the Lumière screening in December 1895 ultimately made irrelevant their attempts to establish the Cinématographe as the exclusive device for moving picture taking and reproducing. The irrepressible tidal wave of competitors that swamped their chosen strategy was very similar to the one that undermined Edison's later attempts to control the motion picture business with the Motion Picture Patents Company in the period 1908–15. The Société A. Lumière et fils was not, after all, a firm with any capacity for mechanical manufacture: that work on the Cinématographe was farmed out to Jules Carpentier in Paris. After 1900 the Lumières were largely inactive in moving pictures except for continuing to distribute their pioneering films and, finally, selling raw stock.

A very different strategy was adopted by Robert Paul in England, whose projection apparatus, the Theatrograph, was publicly sold and in use even before Paul himself had arranged his own first public screenings with his own machine. Unlike Birt Acres (see chapter 5), Paul was largely inactive in moving pictures in the second half of 1895, apart from continuing to manufacture and exhibit his replica kinetoscopes. Inspired by reports of Lumière's work, Paul turned his attention to making a projection apparatus very early in 1896, which he accomplished within weeks and demonstrated at his alma mater, the Finsbury Technical College, on February 20, 1896, the same day that Felicien Trewey gave an invitational press showing of the Cinématographe at the Regent Street Polytechnic in London. Paul's first Theatrograph used a seven-sided spur gear, a variant Maltese cross, to drive a sprocket wheel mounted below the projection aperture while two rollers held the 35 mm film with four sprockets per frame (the same as used in the Kinetoscope and the Paul-Acres film productions). The Theatrograph was clearly meant for sale, as Paul circulated his own handbill describing it to prominent photographic journals. "The apparatus is simple," wrote *The English Mechanic* on February 21, 1896, "and can be adapted to any lantern" (p. 11), while the *British Journal of Photography* commented a week later "If the theatrograph, together with a series of kinetoscopic photographs, is available at reasonable prices, it should supply an extremely popular addition to the resources of the lantern lecturer" (February 28, 1896, p. 143).

Paul improved his Theatrograph in a matter of only a few weeks, adding a continuous-feed sprocket wheel above the projector's aperture and making his intermittent into a double-spur gear linked to two seven-sided Maltese cross–type gears driving film sprockets both above and below the projection gate; this allowed a smoother running machine on which an exhibitor could mount more than two or three film subjects at once, and gave a more secure movement to the film (Paul 1896). A rotary film perforator made by Paul at about the same time, which also used the double-spur intermittent movement, may also have improved the projector's overall performance by giving his film bands more precisely positioned and regular perforations. The result, in any case, was the most influential early projection apparatus in the world next to the Lumière Cinématographe, an influence that came not because it was a decisively superior machine, but because it was for sale.

One of the first Theatrographs was sold to the magician David Devant, who introduced the machine at the Egyptian Hall in London in the magic show he shared with John Nevil Maskelyne on March 19, just two days before Paul gave his own initial public performance at the Olympia Theatre on March 21. Devant served as a kind of early agent for the Theatrograph, and it was he who arranged a sale, also in March, to his colleague magician Georges Méliès, who used it at his Théâtre Robert Houdin in Paris on April 4. Another March sale was to the magician Carl Hertz, who left immediately for South Africa and opened his Theatrograph in Johannesburg on May 9. Also in March 1896, or perhaps early April, a copy of the Paul Theatrograph was brought for repairs to the Berlin optical workshop of Oskar Messter, who had been unsuccessfully trying to make a projection apparatus; Messter copied the Paul intermittent in his own first projectors available from June, launching the film career of the most important pioneer in Germany. Meanwhile, Georges Méliès in Paris had acquired a projector made by Louis Charles (Charles 1896) whose design he later re-patented with two colleagues (Korsten, Méliès, and Reulos 1896; Mannoni 1997a); this allowed him to convert his Theatrograph into a motion picture camera, today preserved at the Cinémathèque française, with which he made his first films in the area around

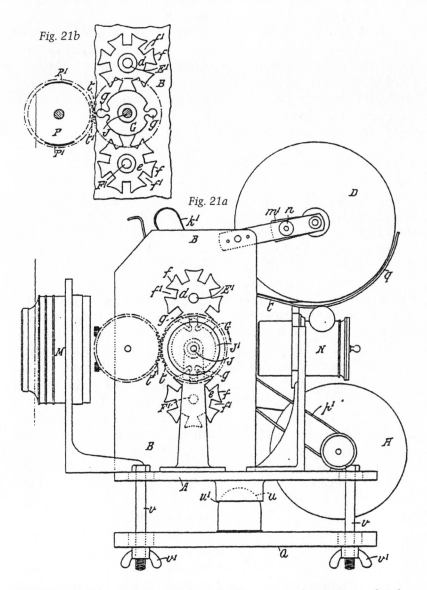

Fig. 21b

Fig. 21a

FIGURE 21. The second model of the Theatrograph projector of Robert William Paul, with its projection lens M at the left, 1896. The double spur gear intermittent is shown in Fig. 21b.

Le Havre and Trouville in July, beginning one of the most important filmmaking careers in early cinema.

Back in London, Robert Paul organized screenings in several theaters around the city and continued to manufacture Theatrographs at his electrical instrument workshops in Hatton
Garden. He later estimated that he had made about a hundred
machines, and by August 1896, the Theatrograph was in wide
use across Great Britain, and it was as well in the hands of showmen exhibiting in France, Spain, South Africa, Portugal, Sweden, Italy, Germany, and Australia (see Rossell 1995 for specific
dates, cities, and exhibitors). Paul built his first film camera in
the spring of 1896 (aside from his earlier work for Birt Acres)
using an intermittent movement based on his second Theatrograph, and returned to film production in April, shooting actu-
alities and a short comedy, *The Soldier's Courtship*, along with
a film of the 1896 Derby that was on the screen in London
within twenty-four hours of the finish of the race.

Paul never established a formal system of employee-opera-
tors like the Lumière brothers, but there are nonetheless some
similarities in his operations: he sent Henry Short to Portugal
and Spain in September, where Short made fourteen films that
he first used in exhibitions in Portugal and that were then added
to Paul's growing catalog of subjects for distribution. Other
exhibitors relied on Paul's growing stock of films including the
original Paul/Acres productions to renew their programs as they
travelled across Scandinavia (A. J. Gee), around the Iberian Pen-
ninsula (Edwin Rousby), or South Africa and Australia (Carl
Hertz). In his first full year of motion picture work, to March
1897, Paul declared a net profit of £6,585. from the manufacture
and sale of cinema equipment and films (Barnes 1983, 8). Never
interested in controlling the entirety of the moving picture
business, Paul relied on his manufacturing experience and
capacity and made most of his profit from sales of apparatus to
others. In doing so, he greatly influenced the course of early cinema, especially through Oskar Messter in Germany and Georges
Méliès in France, although his own assistants G. H. Cricks, J. H.
Martin, Jack Smith, and Walter Booth all had substantial careers
in the cinema in Britain after leaving his shop. Paul continued
to manufacture all types of moving picture equipment until
1910, when he left the film business and concentrated again on

the manufacture of scientific instruments. Considered the founder of the British film industry, Paul was important as a manufacturer, exhibitor, filmmaker, and producer; his business sense was acute and he was hardworking as well: at a later point he recalled dashing between 1896 engagements in London in a one-horse brougham, rewinding films for the next show while in transit (Paul 1936, 44). His hands-on approach was far from that of the American inventor most publicly involved in the beginnings of the cinema projection, Thomas Edison.

Edison's role in the moving picture world of 1896 is a great anomaly. With all of his inventive resources, he achieved projection only by buying up the Phantoscope of Jenkins and Armat. After the debut of this apparatus in New York City on April 23, 1896, at Koster & Bial's Music Hall, it reached Canada only in July, Australia in August, and Europe barely in the autumn. At the same time, throughout this first full year of projected movies, the name of Edison is everywhere associated with the marvellous new invention. His towering presence as the symbol of a modern age of invention, creating wondrous new appliances for both industry and the home, made Edison easily the most recognizable figure in the entire field, even though his personal involvement was negligible and his manufacturing operations significant only in America, where Edison actively wielded broadly drawn patents and influenced the course of the equipment manufacturing industry.

Perhaps the most striking characteristic of moving picture work before 1900 is its fully international character, with a remarkably rapid dissemination of rumor and information, technical developments, wandering exhibitors, and circulation of films themselves across national, linguistic, and cultural borders. Within a select circle that included inventors, mechanics, lanternists, impresarios, and a variety of opportunists, any news of new developments in moving pictures travelled with extreme rapidity. Edison, notwithstanding his direct contacts over the years with Muybridge and Marey, and his experiments with Anschütz apparatus, was somehow still apart from much of this interchange. No one brought him a machine to repair, and he disdained jumping to copy or improve the moving picture apparatus or ideas of others, as he clearly could have done the day after the very first press screening of the Latham Eidoloscope in

April 1895. In the end, it was Edison's chief Kinetoscope agents, Raff & Gammon, who brought the great inventor into contact with movie projection.

Thomas Armat, working apart from C. Francis Jenkins after the presentation of their Phantoscope at the Cotton States Exhibition in Atlanta, arranged a demonstration of the machine in December 1895 for Frank R. Gammon. The Kinetoscope business had been in serious decline for half a year, and Armat later recalled that Raff & Gammon "had been endeavoring for months to have Mr. Edison produce for them a successful machine" for projecting pictures. Gammon stated that Edison "had not been able to produce such a machine, and that he did not believe that anyone else could. When he saw the exhibition he was very much astonished, and the result of our interview on that occasion was the contract under which his firm undertook to exploit the invention" (Musser 1990, 105). In mid-January, Raff and Gammon met with Edison and his business manager William Gilmore, obtaining Edison's permission to use his name in promoting the film projection device. Edison workshops would manufacture the apparatus and royalties would be shared with both Armat and Raff & Gammon. The next month the Phantoscope was renamed the Vitascope, henceforth invariably known as the Edison Vitascope.

As they prepared to launch the Vitascope, Raff & Gamon suggested to Armat that he increase the width of film used in the apparatus beyond the 35 mm Kinetoscope size used in the Phantoscope. "The object in making it wider," they explained, "is not to show scenery, but simply to enable us to make a picture of proper width to exhibit on a theatrical stage. As you yourself heard while here, the criticism made by all the theatrical people is that the picture is too narrow in its width" (Musser 1990, 111). Feeling the same urgency to move forward quickly that had propelled Antoine Lumière, Armat declined to redesign his machine, saying that any changes would take time and necessitate experiments; if desirable, changes could be made later. In retrospect, this was a crucial decision in relation to the rapid growth of the nascent film business: it meant that the marketing skills of Raff & Gammon and the weight of Edison's worldwide reputation would stand behind an apparatus that could use extant 35 mm, four-perforation Kinetoscope films that

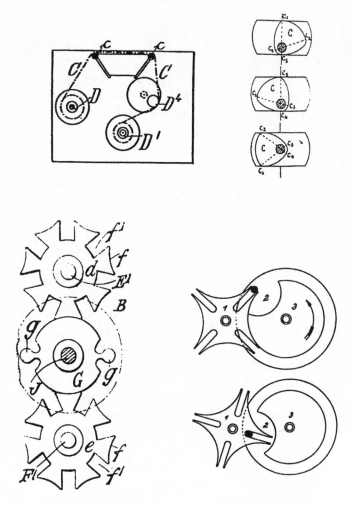

FIGURE 22. Four intermittent movements: top left, the Demenÿ beater movement, also used in the Edison/Armat Vitascope until 1897; top right, the cam-and-box movement for the Lumière Cinématograph, in three positions; bottom left, the Paul double-spur intermittent also used in the first machines of Oskar Messter in Germany; bottom right, a four-sided Maltese Cross movement.

were already in wide circulation and for which, by April 1896, there were already several other makers of projection machines, mostly in Europe.

The Edison Vitascope had its public debut on April 23, 1896, at Koster & Biall's Music Hall in New York City, whose progressive management had installed an Anschütz Electrical Schnellseher at their premises as early as 1892. Two Vitascopes were used, each running a film subject in an endless loop, repeated several times while a new film was mounted on the alternate machine. The films on the opening program included the Kinetoscope productions *Barbershop Scene*, the finale from the play *The Milk White Flag*, the burlesque boxers Walton and Slavin from the play *1492*, and two hand-tinted films, *Umbrella Dance* and *Serpentine Dance*. In addition, Robert Paul supplied a print of the Birt Acres film *Rough Seas at Dover*. News of the screening was carried across the country by a press enthusiastic about Edison's latest invention, and Raff & Gammon's carefully orchestrated sales of states' rights territories meant that the Vitascope opened throughout the United States as soon as Edison's factory had the first group of machines ready in mid-May. But manufacturing progress was slow, and by October 1896 only seventy-three Vitascopes had been finished, although Edison's reputation had received another huge boost from the excitement caused by audiences astounded by the living pictures associated with his name.

Although they held worldwide rights in the Vitascope, Raff & Gammon seem not to have made any significant inroads into Europe with the apparatus. John Barnes found no evidence of the machine's use in England during 1896, and there are only rare appearances of it in Italy, Portugal, Hungary, and Australia late in that year, possibly due to the great demand for machines from American exhibitors combined with the slow construction rate at West Orange. Yet Edison's name is everywhere associated with the new medium, as represented by unidentified equipment showing a "Programma Edison" in Udine, Italy, "Edison's Living Photographs" in Lübeck, Germany, and "Edison's newest phenomenal invention" in Prague, Czech Republic, all advertised in October 1896 (Rossell 1995, 168–70). This might be partly explained by the many Kinetoscope films in circulation, both sold directly by Edison agents and duplicated by others, that "allowed" the mixing-in of Edison's name to almost any exhibition program (although Birt Acres films were shown in Lübeck), and by the currency of Edison's name in the entertainment world due to the circumstance that his phonograph reached an apogee of public exploitation and circulation beginning in 1895 and 1896, well after its official date of invention in 1877 (see Chew 1981, 19–20).

That Edison's name was a valuable and exploitable property in the moving picture world of the mid-1890s is also illustrated by the clever campaign designed by H. O. Foersterling in Berlin, one of the many entrepreneurs who leapt into the film business in 1896, although his interesting career has somewhat deeper roots than many of his colleagues in this "second generation" of moving picture manufacturers. A phonograph pirate and manufacturer of advertising novelties, Foersterling was the technical expert who advised the Stollwerck company to proceed with the purchase of German rights to the Edison phonograph in April 1895, and in August of the same year signed a contract to make films for Stollwerck with a camera supplied by Birt Acres, although it is not yet known if the apparatus was either supplied or used at that time. By April 1896, Foersterling had begun to manufacture film projection apparatus that he at first called the Biomatograph; by June his apparatus became a copy of a machine designed by Pierre-Victor Continsouza in Paris and unpatented in Germany, and was called Edison's Ideal. Foersterling created an advertising campaign and press materials for it that were widely used by exhibitors of his apparatus in Germany, Poland, the Netherlands, Italy, and the Austro-Hungarian empire. This carefully structured campaign, a rarity in the rough-and-tumble world of early film exhibition, associated his device with the work of Edison, Lumière, and Paul, but the machine was always prominently called "Edison's Ideal" to the public (see Rossell 1997).

Foersterling was only one of many manufacturers, exhibitors, and journalists who invoked the magic name of Edison throughout 1896 and later, giving the Wizard of Menlo Park a vivid presence in early cinema far surpassing the reality of his operations. Yet it was Edison's reputation, his identification with moving pictures, with success, and with dynamic new appliances that undoubtedly made a major contribution to the welcome moving pictures received among both audiences and an active generation of impresarios before the turn of the century. Through the spring of 1897 Robert Paul probably built and sold more moving picture apparatus than Edison, and the Lumière brothers exhibited more widely throughout the world, but it was Edison's reputation (along with his Kinetoscope and early film productions) that prepared the ground and infiltrated the public consciousness wherever moving pictures were seen.

The years between 1896 and 1900 saw scores of additional manufacturers, filmmakers, and exhibitors enter the burgeoning industry, many with their own ideas and dreams of what the cinema could be and how its future would develop. It was their competition that ultimately drove the Lumières from the field, and caused Edison to agree to sell all his motion picture interests to the American Mutoscope and Biograph Company in April 1900, an arrangement that failed only when the deal's financing was not successfully concluded. This competition was not primarily a struggle for dominance in a single market, but rather a struggle to define just what moving pictures actually were, how and where they would be seen and used, whether their technology would be in the hands of specialists or a mass public, and what would be the appropriate method for their circulation and promotion. Projected moving pictures now existed in a form far beyond the Choreutoscope, the Praxinoscope, and the persistence of vision toys of earlier decades in the century. As the 1890s came to an end, many technological alternatives were proposed for a medium that would become a stablized industry only after the turn of the century.

Late in 1896 Auguste and Louis Lumière patented another, quite different, cinema apparatus: the Kinora. In relation to their own filmmaking work and the unique way the Cinématographe was presented during this first year of moving pictures, the Kinora reinforces the idea that the Lumières intended moving pictures to be a home or amateur apparatus that would extend their primary business of manufacturing and selling photographic plates and films. The Kinora was a miniature mutoscope viewer operated by a simple clockwork motor (Lumiere 1896). Inside a wooden cabinet 7 inches high, 5 inches wide, and 5 inches deep ran a 5-inch-diameter roll of up to 640 paper leaves $3/4$ inch wide containing photographs transferred from moving picture film and viewed through a magnifying lens 2½ inches long and 1¼ inches wide. Costing fifty francs in 1900, the Kinora showed about forty seconds of moving images. Like the Cinématographe, it was an elegant piece of machinery, not only rugged and stable but also compact and practical: the Kinora was clearly a home-use machine for the individual viewing of motion pictures. At first commercialized by the Gaumont Com-

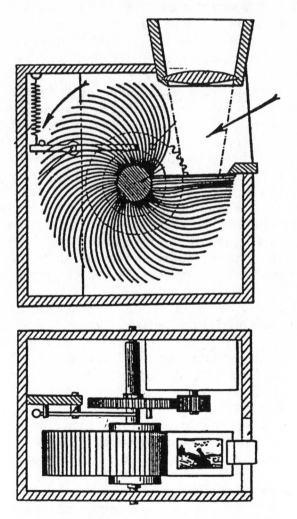

FIGURE 23. The Lumière Kinora as it was originally proposed in the patent of 1896.

pany, the Lumières ultimately drew up a contract with Herman Casler in America for the exploitation of the apparatus, and when relaunched in England from about 1902 by Charles Urban and his Warwick Trading Company, then one of the leading film companies in Britain, the Kinora became extremely popular. Some 700 films, including those made by Lumière, Robert Paul, and others were available for several table-top and hand-held models of Kinora viewers, most now with the reel mounted horizontally and a sturdy, simple gearing for a hand crank. A Kinora camera was available from 1908, and Urban franchised a Kinora portrait service through main street photographers (the most complete histories are Herbert 1984, 1991, and Anthony 1996).

The later experience of the Kinora fulfilled the prophecy of a journalist for *La Poste* writing about the first public exhibition of the Lumière Cinématographe in December 1895: "When these cameras become available to the public, when all are able to photograph their dear ones, no longer merely in immobile form but in movement, in action, with their familiar gestures, with speech on their lips, death will no longer be final" (Chardère 1995, 315). The early films of Louis Lumière, taken during the year 1895, are predominantly domestic scenes and views of ordinary events that have strong resonances with the home movie practices of today: *La Sortie d'usine* (Workers Leaving the Factory), *Les Forgerons* (The Blacksmiths), *Le Repas* (Feeding the Baby), *Récréation à la Martinière* (Playtime at Martinière), *Baignade en mer* (Bathing at the Sea), *Barque sortant du port* (Boat Leaving Harbor), *Partie d'écarte* (The Card Party). One of the most widely known of the Lumière films, also made by Louis but a year later, *Arrivée d'un train à La Ciotat*, was again principally a home movie: the station platform is populated by several members and retainers of the Lumière family, awaiting the arrival of two of the Lumière children; in one of those accidents so beloved by filmmakers in ensuing years, however, the train stopped in the wrong place and the children, who were not fully cooperative, are barely glimpsed at the end of the film (Loiperdinger 1996).

These are some of the many indications that Louis Lumière thought that the principal site of moving pictures would be the home, and that his essential motivation for working on the Cinématographe was the benefit that would accrue to his company through selling a generation of enthusiastic amateur film-makers their basic supply of celluloid film stock. The design simplicity of the Cinématographe and the personal film career of Louis Lumière suggest the direction of his thinking about moving pictures, and the appearance of his next moving picture device, the Kinora, confirms it. But by the end of the century it was clear that despite the unique library of films that their many Cinématographe operators had created during their travels around the world, the Lumière filmed documents were being surpassed by a new and articulate moving picture language based on editing and photographic magic, and that the dangers of highly flammable celluloid film prevented their system from being used widely in the home or by amateurs, just as other proposals for less expensive celluloid-based moving pictures were inhibited by its flammability, such as the 17.5 mm apparatus of Birt Acres with his Birtac camera and projector of 1898 and the Biokam of the same year designed by Alfred Darling and Alfred Wrench for the Warwick Trading Company (Acres 1898; Darling and Wrench 1898). The major proposals for home cinema would come from inventors who abandoned fiery celluloid to return, ingeniously, to glass plate photography.

When Pierre-Victor Continsouza and René Bünzli patented a cinema apparatus in France in November 1896, the photographic images were recorded on a glass plate, and they confidently predicted the end of celluloid moving pictures (Continsouza and Bünzli 1896). Their apparatus substituted a circular glass plate for flexible celluloid film, with the images arranged on it in a spiral; the glass plate itself was moved intermittently by a four-sided Maltese Cross. Leonard Ulrich Kamm manufactured his widely used Kammatograph combination camera and projector from 1900, which also used a circular glass plate (Kamm 1898); the Kammatograph held 550 exposures arranged in a spiral on a twelve-inch-diameter disk. Similar apparatus was proposed by the Bettini Brothers in 1897, whose Plattenkinematograph held 576 images; in England the Spirograph of Henry W. Joy patented in 1907 was marketed by Charles Urban, who also supplied owners with ready-made glass disks whose subjects were taken from his large distribution catalog. In France, the Olikos apparatus of 1912 used multiple square glass plates each holding 49 frames 7 by 8 mm. The patent for a glass-disk apparatus of Robert Krayn from 1897 is straightforward about the use and attraction of these machines: "The purpose of this invention is to give amateur photographers the possibility of making series photographs, in particular by the least costly means on light sensitive round plates" (Krayn 1897, 1).

The very small images of these glass-plate machines, their consequently small apertures, and the limited intensity of the light source that could be used in projection meant that these machines were limited to use in a family setting, or for showings to small, intimate groups. A marketing advantage was their reliance on the considerable expertise of both amateur and professional or semiprofessional photographers in exposing, developing, handling, and storing glass plates. By using such a familiar material that could be processed and treated in a manner well within the experience of many photographers, makers of glass-plate cinematography apparatus hoped to find a ready market for their goods. Along with this preexistent familiarity, glass also had the advantage of using nonflammable materials, unlike the more dangerous and frightening celluloid bands used in other apparatus.

Apart from safety considerations, another advantage of glass-plate cinematography for an individual market was that the cost of operating a glass-plate machine was considerably less than the expense of either a 35 mm celluloid apparatus or one using a celluloid film of reduced dimensions. At the turn of the century, it was estimated in Germany that the Bettini Plattenkinematograph, which held 576 images, provided the equivalent of about 11 meters of 35-mm celluloid film. At 80 pfennig the meter, a film negative cost 8.80 marks, and the equally long positive film needed for projection cost an additional 8. 80 marks. A glass-plate negative for the Bettini machine cost 15 pfennig, with the required positive plate adding another 15 pfennig, adding up to a total cost of only 30 pfennig for glass-plate cinematography with the equivalent screen time of celluloid film costing 17.60 marks (Rossell 1995, 216). The Plattenkinematograph, like most of the glass-plate apparatus, held about forty seconds of moving pictures, somewhat longer than a Lumière film and a bit shorter than the average turn-of-the-century film subject.

The cinema as a portable medium of visual instruction or entertainment that extended the traditions of magic lantern shows is one that was represented technologically by almost all of the equipment that came onto the market from 1896, with the exception of a few large machines specially designed for semipermanent installation in large halls or theaters. Many of the first generation of cinema inventors and manufacturers had experience in making magic lantern equipment or as magic lantern showmen, categories that were often blurred as showmen relied on a thorough grounding in projection technology for their work, which demanded a highly developed knowledge of illuminants and special slide-changing apparatus, among other skills. The generation of moving picture inventors and manufacturers who arrived on the scene at the beginning of 1896 also included many figures who were already active in the magic lantern world, and their background was transferred to the apparatus that they designed and built as they conceived of moving pictures as the next on-screen "effect" for the lantern. Their thinking was so deeply situated in a technological frame of magic lantern practice that along with a repertoire of films drawn from lantern stories and images they also carried over longstanding traditions of lantern work into the mechanics of their moving picture apparatus.

Such wholesale transference of thinking from the magic lantern to moving pictures is nowhere more strikingly revealed than in the Hughes Street Cinematograph, which reached the market in 1898. The patented apparatus was nothing less than a portable projector and theater combined (Hughes 1898). It provided a self-contained, collapsible environment for exhibiting movies without the need for renting a hall or waiting for darkness. Advertised as "the greatest money-making novelty of the nineteenth century," the Hughes Street Cinematograph consisted of a trapezoidal case nine feet long and three feet wide at its larger end. Eight viewing ports jutted out from each side of the wooden case, which was set on two sawhorses or trestles. Each of the sixteen peep holes gave a clear view of a three foot wide screen set in a proscenium at the wider end (a Duplex model allowed forty people to view the projections). Opposite the screen and fully enclosed in a smaller wooden case was a Hughes Photo-Rotoscope 35-mm projector using a three-wick oil lamp for illumination. An extra pair of peep holes was provided for the operator of the machine; the projected film ran into an enclosed vertical cabinet below the lens. The entire contraption was fitted together with bolts, and according to the manufacturers could be set up or broken down in just five minutes.

A former magician, entertainer, and dentist, William Charles Hughes was an optician and lantern manufacturer from 1871 who held many patents for improvements in lanterns, illuminants, slide-changers, and other lantern accessories. Among his many creations were quick-change lantern slide devices (Hughes 1886), a slide magazine for storing the images for an

FIGURE 24. The Street Cinematograph of W. C. Hughes, from an 1898 illustration.

entire show at the projector, and several powerful lamps and special feed valves for illuminating gases. In 1884 he repopularized the Beale Choreutoscope as the Giant Choreutoscope (Hughes 1884), which allowed larger images to be used in the intermittently driven mechanical slide (which was also sometimes called a Phantoscope). His Docwra Triple Lantern, which won the only prize medal for lanterns at the 1893 Crystal Palace Exhibition, was one of the most elaborate Triunial (three-stage) dissolving magic lanterns, a magnificent creation of mahogany and brass that represented the state of the art in lantern projection. By 1897 Hughes had added both films and moving picture apparatus to his large catalog of goods, at first machines made by the Prestwich Manufacturing Company, but by the following year apparatus of his own design using a beater movement. The Photo-Rotoscope that was used in his peep-show portable theater was intended by Hughes for use not only in his Street Cinematograph but also in smaller halls or at home; it was somewhat lighter and more compact than other machines in his line of offerings. According to John Barnes (1983, 159), another type of street cinematograph that extended the old traditions of peep-show exhibitions was also available in England in 1897: manufactured in Chicago and offered by the Eclipse Kinematoscope Office in London, it was small enough to be carried from place to place by a single man.

Most of the W. C. Hughes apparatus of the period was easily convertible to showing slides or still images; in the case of his larger Motor-Pictoroscope, the intermittent and feed mechanism was mounted on the side door of the projector, and opening the door left the optics in place so that slides could be projected as film titles, or while the film subject was changed. Many other early machines were also quickly covertible to the projection of magic lantern slides, including apparatus made in England by J. Otway and Sons, where a mirror at the condenser redirected light to a slide stage and lens next to the film mechanism, and the Warwick Trading Company, where the film path and intermittent racked sideways and was replaced on the machine's optical axis by an alternate slide stage and lens. The practice of making combination slide and moving picture projectors continued until about 1910, but one of the most remarkable machines was in use mainly before 1900: the Riley Kinetoptoscope of 1896.

156

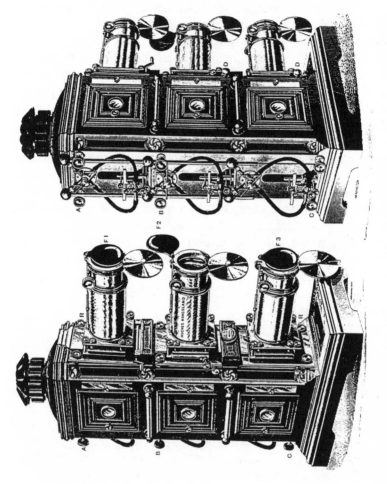

FIGURE 25. The Docwra triple lantern of 1888, designed by Colin Docwra and made by W. C. Hughes of London.

The Riley Brothers advertised as "The Largest Lantern Outfitters in the World" and offered a full range of lanterns, photographic goods, and over 1,500 sets of slides for sale or rental from their main offices in Bradford and branches in London and New York City (Gordon 1980, 32–33). Their elegant small projector had been designed by Cecil Wray in the spring of 1896 and was marketed by them from November after they bought out the inventor's patent (Wray 1896). *The Optical Magic Lantern Journal* described the overall concept of the machine saying, "The apparatus is separate and distinct from the lantern itself, and can be applied to any lantern provided with a tolerably wide stage. The appliance is merely pushed in after the style of a slide" (November 1896, 194). The Kineoptoscope used no sprocket wheels, a four-pin claw intermittent movement being sufficient to draw down each frame of the film past the optical axis of the lantern. By early 1897 it was also offered as a freestanding model that could be slid in front of a lantern and fastened on a short flanged track. The Kineoptoscope can be seen as the ultimate development of the mechanical lantern slide, providing full moving pictures from the lantern slide stage. The interchangeability of lantern projection and film projection is physically and conceptually expressed in no better example.

Magic lantern practice had a negative effect on yet another branch of emerging moving picture technology: the production of apparatus with continuously moving film bands and optical intermittents, instead of mechanical ones. Apart from the continuously moving film of the Edison Kinetoscope, which was not a projection device but viewed directly, a number of inventors proposed optical projection systems before 1900, among the earliest being those of Paul Mortier in France and John Neville Maskelyne in England (Mortier 1896; Maskelyne 1896). Even the Lumière brothers patented an optical-intermittent projector using continuously moving film just after the turn of the century, when most histories consider them to have abandoned all moving picture work (Lumière 1902). Optical systems had several clear advantages over devices using mechanical intermittent movements, since they did not stop and start the fragile celluloid film sixteen or more times a second. As a consequence, there was no tearing of sprocket holes, and little wear to the surface of the film that carried the image. Contemporary accounts of film exhibitions until well after 1900 constantly complain about the state of the prints in use: scratched, torn, and scarred films were ordinarily used until they literally fell apart in projection. Optical systems promised not only better-quality film shows, but also less frequent replacement of the showman's most expensive recurring investment. From one perspective, optical intermittents and continuous movement should have been privileged as the cinema was born: the Praxinoscope of Reynaud had successfully used rotating mirrors to supply intermittency to its images since 1877, and his Théâtre Optique was arguably the most successful precinema public screen projection of images, an example that attracted great crowds beginning in 1892 and continuing until 1900.

Maskelyne's optical system projector, which he called the Mutagraph and which featured a combination of rotating and fixed lenses, was in use from sometime in 1897 in his regular shows at the Egyptian Hall in London, where it apparently remained successfully in place for many years (Barnes 1976, 155–57); adapted for high-speed work, an example was in use by the British artillery-testing commission at the Woolwich Arsenal as late as 1908 (Liesegang 1908, 744). W. K. L. Dickson, Anton Musger, the American Mutoscope and Biograph Company, and others patented early optical systems, but most of the dozens of proposals for continuously moving film and optical intermittents came after 1900 and outside the scope of this study, as does the most successful apparatus, the projector of Emil Mechau, first patented in 1912 and manufactured in over 500 copies between 1921 and 1934, at first by Leitz-Kinowerke in Rastatt, and then by AEG in Berlin.

The long-lasting search for a usable optical approach to moving picture projection was a reflection that even as cinema technology stabilized after 1905, the short life of film prints and the distress caused to audiences by worn films were a continuing problem of high priority. Why, then, were optical systems not successful at the beginning? Liesegang (1908, 744) gives one reason when he states that the British army's high-speed Maskelyne apparatus had cost in the neighborhood of £10,000. But the main obstacle to the successful introduction of optical intermittent systems was a negative side-effect of the linkage of moving pictures with magic lantern practice. In the sophisticated development of magic lantern illuminants and lenses for projection in the second half of the nineteenth century, showmen were perfectly satisfied that they had an existing optical system that was both refined in its precision and flexible in its application to large or small auditoriums. In the prevailing view, what was needed was a mechanically faster way of changing the images ("slides") so that the perceptual effect of continuous motion was present for a viewer. As we have seen in the development of the Kineoptoscope, the Theatrograph, and many other early devices, moving pictures were a logical and easily understood new attachment to the magic lantern. With audiences initially excited by the lifelike representations of the new marvel, it did not seem crucial to develop a whole new optical delivery system that revived already-solved problems of proper illumination, focus, and image clarity. The magic lantern was a reliable instrument with many experienced users, who could concentrate their attention on any foibles present in their moving picture accessory and not have to learn an entirely new system of presentation.

Moving picture apparatus intended for use in large theaters developed yet another technical solution for taking and projecting living pictures, and its leading exponent before 1900, the American Mutoscope and Biograph Company (AM&B), also adopted a business strategy particularly well suited to its technology. When the K.C.M.D. group turned to making a projector, they already possessed a camera used to make films whose $2^3/_4$ inch wide images were cut up for the manufacture of Mutoscope reels (Casler 1896). They also thought the unique friction plate intermittent of this camera was not an infringement on Edison's patents, although epic legal battles were to be fought on this question well past the turn of the century. It was a natural development that their projector should use the same size film and another friction intermittent, even though this posed additional problems in continually adjusting the flow of the film at the projection aperture to correct for the slight irregularities caused by the gripper intermittent. The unique adjustment that W. K. L. Dickson most likely suggested for Herman Casler's Biograph projector was an extention of an idea he used in the intermittent of the Kinetograph camera. For Edison's intermittent, Dickson provided a constantly driven notched wheel on which a second wheel with bent teeth and driven by a friction belt bore at right angles. As the teeth of the second wheel dropped through the constantly appearing slots of the first, intermittent movement was given to the film for exposure in the Kinetograph. In the new arrangement for the AM&B apparatus, intermittent movement was provided by two wide counterrotating disks each cut away so that about a third of their surface protruded to make simultaneous contact on either side of the celluloid film, bringing a new frame into the aperture of the projector at each revolution of the disks (Casler 1896a, 1896b). In Dickson's adjustment, in order to finely regulate the framing of a moving film during projection, its speed through the apparatus needed to be corrected from time to time, independent of the constant movement of the gripper intermittent, and his solution was a clutch arrangement consisting of another pair of right-angled disks, one driven constantly and the second, connected to the feed sprockets, capable of moving toward the center of the first disk (slower) or toward its outer edge (faster).

Although the Biograph apparatus was a piece of technology that was significantly more complex than most other machines in use in 1897–98, needing an alert and attentive operator, its results on the screen were superior in both picture quality and clarity, according to most contemporary reports. AM&B films lasted for the same minute or so as those of their competitors, but the large $2^{3}/_{4}$ inch wide image ran at about thirty frames per second and therefore were some 250 feet long. The extra speed reduced flicker (as it had done in the Kinetoscope) and the oversize image was particularly suited to large-screen presentations. Comparably, the AM&B technology had the same effects in relation to normal 35 mm film as Douglas Trumbull's Showscan process, with its 70 mm film driven at sixty frames per second has today: both produced startlingly vivid images on a large screen. With the entire mechanism and its feed and take-up reels, plus the electric arc illumination fitted in an asbestos-lined compartment, all surrounded by a huge wooden cabinet, the Biograph projector was hardly portable. It was also not for sale, and intended for exhibition in large vaudeville and varieté theaters, who rented a complete service, including the machine, an operator, and changing film programs from the parent company AM&B. One machine was in use at Keith's Union Square

Theater from January 18, 1897 until eight and a half years later on July 15, 1905 (Hendricks 1964, 51).

The first engagements for the new Biograph system were with a vaudeville company featuring the strongman Eugene Sandow in a program called "Sandow's Olympia," with the films shown at the conclusion of the evening. Sandow and the Biograph played for a week in Pittsburgh from September 14, followed by Philadelphia (September 21), Brooklyn (September 28), and ended at the Grand Opera House in New York on October 10 (Rossell 1995, 165–68). From AM&B's still limited stock of film subjects, the tour exhibited several scenes of Joseph Jefferson in his most famous role as *Rip Van Winkle, Stable on Fire, A Hard Wash*, and films of Sandow himself. On October 12, the Biograph reopened at Hammerstein's Olympia Theater in a gala event that was also a political rally for the Republican Party that featured new films of candidate William McKinley at home in Canton, Ohio. The press reports were rapturous, particularly noting the lack of flicker and the steadiness of the large Biograph pictures on the screen. By the end of the year AM&B had a contract with impresario B. F. Keith to supply machines for his major vaudeville houses across the East Coast and the company was firmly established as a significant American producer and exhibitor. Over the next three years AM&B established subsidiary firms in England, Germany, and elsewhere, again relying on their unique technology to exhibit in large theaters and becoming a major international producer.

That the size of the image was central to successful presentation in large theaters is clear from Raff & Gammon's approach to Thomas Armat to increase the size of film used in his Vitascope, noted previously. Several other manufacturers produced apparatus using wide film during this period, among them the Gaumont Chronophotographe, the development of a Georges Demenÿ apparatus using 60 mm film, but none had the full production system and clear business plan of the AM&B, which remained the outstanding large-size projector well past the turn of the century. By choosing to work with large theatrical enterprises, AM&B had married the amusement world's establishment, removing for them all worries about film supply, installation and operation of the equipment, and reliability of its operation. Their success in this world helped moving picture technology stabilize and prosper in the world of fixed theater exhibition.

The Biograph's complex technology had come a long way from the continuously runing forty-two-foot film loops of the Edison Kinetoscope. Like Ducos du Hauron in an earlier age, the inventors and mechanics of the late 1890s foresaw many different cinemas, some of which they were not quite able to physically establish. Some attempts failed on mechanical grounds, some on financial grounds, some because a business infrastructure had not yet developed in parallel with the mechanical potential of their devices and inhibited the widespread dispersal of their ideas and apparatus. Nonetheless, most of their ideas would, over time, come into widespread use.

The home cinema of the Lumière brothers became a reality with the introduction of 16 mm and then 8 mm nonflammable films in the 1920s and 1930s, delighting families for decades until it was replaced by home videotape equipment. Continuously moving film bands and optical intermittency was used with great success by scientists, from Étienne-Jules Marey's successor Lucien Bull to Jean Painlève, and is today the basis of the Imax and Omnimax giant screen systems. The cinema rediscovered oversized film formats in the 1950s with the introduction of the Todd-AO, Technirama, CinemaScope 55, Panavision 70, and other systems, encouraged today by the ability of wide film formats to include extra soundtracks for spectacular aural effects.

Through its association at the very beginning with the magic lantern, the first moving picture apparatus entered a secure world of screen entertainment within which it was nurtured and which it slowly surpassed as a public attraction. In fulfilling the dreams of van Musschenbroek and many later lanternists to make pictures move on a screen, and through the efforts of the Lumière brothers to generate worldwide interest in the new medium, the cinema gained a foothold in the world that destroyed its host. Although slide projectors remain both an educational and amateur home apparatus, the public entertainments and scientific lectures of the lantern showmen is but a memory of the past. Modern lanternists travelling today with their mahogany triunials recreate Victorian entertainments as a historical endeavor, frequently astonishing contemporary audiences with the pictorialism of finely painted slides that are valuable collector's items. Few remember that the omnipresent moving pictures that reach a mass public in theaters around the world and enter private homes through television were born as an attachment to the magic lantern. But the passing of the magic lantern, like the later industrialization of moving picture entertainment, was not clearly foreseen in the moment of the cinema's birth. As Louis Lumière was reported to have said in the mid-1930s: "The cinema? I don't go anymore. If I had known what would become of it, I wouldn't have invented it."

BIBLIOGRAPHY

Acres, Birt. 1895. Letter of 6 August 1895 to Ludwig Stollwerck in Cologne, p. 2. Stollwerck Archiv, Cologne. (Also reproduced in facsimile in Lange-Fuchs 1995, 42–43).

———. 1895a. *Improved Apparatus for Enabling Photographic Images to be Taken, Projected, or Viewed in Rapid Succession.* UK patent 10,474. Filed May 27, 1895. Issued May 2, 1896.

———. 1895b. [Paul Müller, agent for Stollwerck & Co] *Vorrichtung zur Aufnahme und Projektion von Reihenbildern.* German patent 92,247. Filed August 25, 1895. Issued June 12, 1897.

———. 1898. *Improvements in Cinematographic Apparatus.* UK patent 12,939. Filed June 9, 1898. Issued June 2, 1899.

Adams, Walter Poynter. 1888. *Improvements in Magic Lantern Slides and Apparatus in Connection therewith.* UK patent 16,785. Filed on November 19, 1888.

Allister, Ray. 1948. *Friese Greene—Close-up of an Inventor.* London: Marshland Publications.

Anderson, Edward L. 1883. *The Gallop.* Edinburgh: David Douglas.

Anderton, John and Alfred Lomax. 1894. *Improvements in Kineto-scopes.* UK patent 25,100. Filed December 27, 1894. Issued October 26, 1895.

Anonymous. 1886. "The Movements of the Heart and Intestines Illustrated by Photography." In *Boston Medical and Surgical Journal* 115.21 (November 25, 1886): 502–3.

Anschütz, Ottomar. 1890. *Stroboskopischer Apparat (Schnellseher)*. German patent 60,285. Filed on November 15, 1890. Issued December 19, 1891.

——. 1890a. [Report of the meeting of the Photographische Verein zu Berlin.] *Photographische Nachrichten* (Berlin), 1890, pp. 68–69.

——. 1894. *Projektionsapparat für stroboskopisch bewegte Bilder*. German patent 85,791. Filed on November 6, 1894. Issued March 7, 1896.

Anthony, Barry. 1996. *Kinora Motion Pictures for the Home, 1896–1914*. London: The Projection Box.

Archer, Frederick Scott. 1855. *Certain Improvements in Photography*. UK patent 1914. Filed on August 24, 1855.

Armat, Thomas. 1896. *Vitascope*. US patent 578,185. Filed on September 26, 1896. Issued March 2, 1897.

Aubert, Michelle and Jean-Claude Seguin. 1996. *La Production Cinématographique des Frères Lumière*. Paris: Editions Mémoirs de cinéma.

Barnes, John. 1976. *The Beginnings of the Cinema in England*. London, David & Charles.

——. 1983. *The Rise of the Cinema in Great Britain*, vol. 2: *The Jubilee Year 1897*. London: Bishopsgate Press Limited.

——. 1985. "The Projected Image: A Short History of Magic Lantern Slides." *The New Magic Lantern Journal* 3.3 (October 1985): 2–7.

Bedts, George William de. 1896. *Système de méchanisme à mouvement intermittent applicable aux appareils chronophotographiques et aux appareils pour projections animées*. French patent 253,195. Filed January 14, 1896.

Bernard, Denis and André Gunthert. 1993. *L'instant rêvé. Albert Londe*. Nîmes: Éditions Jacqueline Chambon/Éditions Laval.

Bessy, Maurice and Lo Duca. 1948. *Louis Lumière, inventeur*. Paris: Éditions Prisma.

Bijker, Wiebe E. 1987. "The Social Construction of Bakelite: Toward a Theory of Invention." In *The Social Construction of Technological Systems*, ed. Wiebe E. Bijker, Thomas P. Hughes, and Trevor Pinch, 159–87. Cambridge, MA: MIT Press.

Bleier-Brody, Agnes. 1960. "Daten zur Urgeschichte des österreichischen Films." *Theater und Film. Referate und Diskussionsbeiträge*, Jahresband 1960 of *Film-Kunst* (Vienna), 27–34.

Bottomore, Stephen. 1996. "Nine Days' Wonder: Early Cinema and its Sceptics." In *Cinema: The Beginnings and the Future*, ed. Christopher Williams. London: Westminster University Press.

Braun, Marta. 1992. *Picturing Time: The Work of Étienne-Jules Marey (1830–1904)*. Chicago/London: University of Chicago Press.

Brown, O. B. 1869. *Optical Instrument*. US Patent 93,594. Issued August 10, 1869.

Carlson, W. Bernard. 1992. "Artifacts and Frames of Meaning: Thomas A. Edison, His Managers, and the Cultural Construction of Motion Pictures." In *Shaping Technology/Building Society: Studies in Sociotechnical Change*, ed. Wiebe E. Bijker and John Law. Cambridge, MA: MIT Press.

Casler, Herman. 1893. *Pocket-Camera*. US patent 509,841. Filed March 1, 1893. Issued November 28, 1893.

———. 1895. *Mutoscope*. US patent 549,309. Filed November 14, 1895. Issued November 5, 1895.

———. 1895a. *Mutoscope*. US patent 584,305. Filed November 14, 1895. Divided and this application filed May 26, 1896. Issued June 8, 1897.

———. 1896. *Kinetographic Camera*. US patent 629,063. Filed February 26, 1896. Issued July 18, 1899.

———. 1896a. *Consecutive View Apparatus*. US patent 666,495. Filed February 26, 1896. Issued January 22, 1901.

———. 1896b. *Consecutive View Apparatus*. US patent 611,591. Filed December 10, 1896. Issued September 27, 1898.

———. 1896c. *Consecutive-View Apparatus*. US patent 597,759. Filed May 28, 1897. Issued January 25, 1898.

Castan, Joachim. 1995. *Max Skladanowsky, oder der Beginn einer deutschen Filmgeschichte*. Stuttgart, Füsslin Verlag.

Chanan, Michael. 1996. *The Dream That Kicks: The Prehistory and Early Years of Cinema in Britain* (2nd ed.). London/New York: Routledge.

Chardère, Bernard. 1985. *Les Lumière* [with Guy and Marjorie Borgé]. Lausanne/Paris: Payot/Bibliothèque des Arts.

———, ed. 1987. *Lumières sur Lumière.* Lyon: Institut Lumière/Presses Universitaires de Lyon.

———. 1995. *Le roman des Lumière.* (Paris: Gallimard).

Charles, Louis Henri. 1896. *Nouveau mode de commande de la pellicule dans la photographie animée.* French patent 255,702. Filed April 20, 1896.

Chew, V. K. 1981. *Talking Machines.* (London, Her Majesty's Stationery Office (Science Museum).

Coe, Brian. 1962. "William Friese Greene and the Origins of Kinematography." *The Photographic Journal* (London), March 1962, pp. 92–104, and April 1962, pp. 121–27.

———. 1978. *Cameras: From Daguerreotypes to Instant Pictures.* Gothenburg: AB Nordbok.

———. 1992. *Muybridge and the Chronophotographers.* London: Museum of the Moving Image.

Conot, Robert. 1979. *A Streak of Luck.* New York: Seaview Books.

Continsouza, Pierre-Victor and René Bünzli. 1896. *Nouvel appareil pour l'obtention et la projection animée.* French patent 261,292. Application 14 November 1896.

Cutting, James A. 1854. *An Improved Process of Taking Photogaphic Pictures upon Glass, and also of Beautifying and Preserving the Same.* UK patent 1638. Filed on July 26, 1854.

Darling, Alfred and Alfred Wrench. 1898. *An Improved Camera and Apparatus for Producing Cinematograph and Other Pictures and for Exhibiting Cinematographic Pictures.* UK patent 23,591. Filed November 9, 1898. Issued August 12, 1899.

David, Ludwig. 1897. *Die Moment-Photographie.* Halle a. S.: Verlag Wilhelm Knapp.

Demenÿ, Georges. 1892. *Un appareil dit phonoscope, reproduisant l'illusion des mouvements de la parole et de la physionomie par vision directe ou par projection au moyen d'une lumière.* French patent 219,830. Filed March 3, 1892.

————. 1893. *Appareil destiné à prendre des séries d'images photographiques à des intervalles de temps égaux et très rapprochés sur une pellicule sensible.* French patent 233,337. Filed October 10, 1893.

————. 1893a. *Un appareil destiné à prendre des séries d'images photographiques à des intervalles de temps égsaux et très rapprochés sur une pellicule sensible.* Swiss patent 7703. Filed December 11, 1893.

————. 1893b. *Serien-Apparat für Aufnahmen auf endlosem Negativband mit einem Objektiv.* German patent 80,424. Filed December 12, 1893. Issued April 1, 1895.

Devant, David. 1931. *My Magic Life.* London: Hutchinson.

Dyer, Frank L. and Thomas C. Martin. 1910. *Edison: His Life and Inventions.* New York: Harper & Brothers.

Eames, Owen A. 1895. *Camera-Lantern.* US patent 546,093. Filed March 25, 1895. Issued September 10, 1895.

————. 1896. "The Animatoscope." *American Photographic Times,* July 1896, pp. 330–31.

Edison, Thomas A. 1891. *Kinetographic Camera.* U.S. Patent 403,534. Filed August 24, 1891. Issued August 31, 1897.

————. 1891a. *Stop Device.* U. S. Patent 403,535. Filed August 24, 1891. Divided and issued as U. S. Patent 491,993 on February 21, 1893.

————. 1891b. *Apparatus for Exhibiting Photographs of Moving Objects.* U.S. Patent 403,536. Filed August 24, 1891. Issued March 14, 1893.

Eastman, George. 1889. *Improvements in Flexible Photographic Film.* US patent 306,284. Filed on April 9, 1889.

Feddersen, Bernhard Wilhelm. 1858. "Beiträger zur Kenntniss des elektrischen Funkens." *Annalen der Physik und Chemie* (Leipzig) 103 (1858).

————. 1908. *Entladung der Leiderner Flasche.* Leipzig: Oswald's Klassiker Nr. 166.

Friedel, Robert. 1983. *Pioneer Plastic: The Making and Selling of Celluloid.* Madison: University of Wisconsin Press.

Friese Greene, William and Mortimer Evans. 1889. *Improved Apparatus for Taking Photographs in Rapid Series*. UK patent 10,131. Filed June 21, 1889. Issued May 10, 1890.

Frizot, Michel. 1984. *La Chronophotographie*. Beaune: Association des amis de Marey et Ministère de la culture).

Goldsmith, J. B. 1922. *Alexander Parkes, Parkesine, Xylonite and Celluloid*. Manuscript, British Library, London.

Goodwin, Hannibal Williston. 1887. *Photographic Pellicule and Process of Producing Same*. US patent 610,861. Filed on May 3, 1887. Issued September 13, 1898.

Gordon, Colin. 1980. *By Gaslight in Winter: A Victorian Family History Through the Magic Lantern*. London: Elm Tree Books.

Gosser, H. Mark. 1988. "The Armat-Jenkins Dispute and the Museums." *Film History* 2.1 (Winter 1988): 1–12.

Gray, Robert Dempsey. 1895. *Series Photographic Camera*. US patent 540,545. Filed March 9, 1895. Issued June 4, 1895.

———. 1895a. *Serien-Apparat mit zwei Filmbändern*. German patent 92,809. Filed June 2, 1895. Issued July 29, 1897.

Haas, Robert Bartlett. 1976. *Muybridge: Man in Motion*. Berkeley/Los Angeles/London: University of California Press.

Hallett, Henry Watson. 1867. *An Improved Mode of and Means for Producing Optical Illusions*. UK patent 629. Issued March 6, 1867.

Harding, Colin. 1995. "Celluloid and Photography: Part One—Celluloid as a Substitute for Glass." *Photographica World* 75: 23–26.

———. 1996. "Celluloid and Photogaphy: Part Two—The Development of Celluloid Rollfilm." *Photographica World* 76: 34–36.

Hecht, Hermann. 1993. *Pre-Cinema History: An Encyclopaedia and Annotated Bibliography of the Moving Image Before 1896*. Edited by Anne Hecht. London/Munich: Bowker/Saur.

Hendricks, Gordon. 1961. *The Edison Motion Picture Myth*. Berkeley/Los Angeles: University of California Press.

———. 1964. *Beginnings of the Biograph: The Story of the Invention of the Mutoscope and the Biograph and their Supplying Camera*. New York: The Beginnings of the American Film.

────. 1966. *The Kinetoscope: America's First Commercially Successful Motion Picture Exhibitor*. New York: The Beginnings of the American Film.

Henry, David. 1984. "York & Son, Part 1." *New Magic Lantern Journal* 3.1 (February 1984): 12–17.

Herbert, Stephen. 1984. *Kinora Living Pictures*. Amateur Cinematography, Paper No. 6. London: The Author.

────. 1991. "Kinora Living Pictures." *Photo Historian* 95 (Winter 1991): 104–13.

Hoffmann, Detlev, and Almut Junker. 1982. *Laterna Magica. Lichtbilder aus Menschenwelt und Götterwelt*. Berlin: Frölich & Kaufmann.

Hough, James Edward. 1895. [Philip M. Justice] *Improvements in Means for Viewing a Series of Pictures for the Purpose of Obtaining from Same an Appearance of Movement*. UK patent 9881. Filed May 18, 1895. Issued April 18, 1896.

Hughes, Thomas P., 1983. *Networks of Power: Electrification in Western Society, 1880–1930*. Baltimore/London: Johns Hopkins University Press.

Hughes, William Charles. 1884. *An Improved Frame for Rapidly Changing the Pictures in a Magic Lantern*. UK patent 13,372. Filed October 9, 1884.

────. 1886. *An Improved Device to Allow of Rapidly Changing the Pictures in a Magic Lantern*. UK patent 9383. Filed July 20, 1886.

Hyatt, John W., Jr. 1869. *Improved Method of Making Solid Collodion*. US patent 91,341. Issued on June 15, 1869.

────. 1884. *Method of and Means for Holding Celluloid and Dividing It into Sheets*. US patent 301,995. Filed on June 10, 1884.

Hyatt, John W., Jr. and Isaiah S. Hyatt. 1870. *Improvement in Treating and Molding Pyroxyline*. US patent 105,338. Filed on July 12, 1870.

Israel, Paul. 1989. "Telegraphy and Edison's Invention Factory." In *Working at Inventing: Thomas A. Edison and the Menlo Park Experience*, ed. William S. Pretzer, 66–83. Dearborn, MI: Henry Ford Museum & Greenfield Village.

Jenkins, C. Francis. 1894. *Phantoscope.* US patent 536,569. Filed November 24, 1894. Issued March 26, 1895.

——. 1894a. *Kinetographic Camera.* US patent 560,800. Filed December 12, 1894. Issued May 26, 1896.

Jenkins, C. Francis and Thomas Armat. 1895. *Phantoscope.* US patent 586,953. Filed August 28, 1895. Issued July 20, 1897.

Jenkins, Reese V. 1975. *Images and Enterprise: Technology and the American Photographic Industry, 1839 to 1925.* Baltimore/London: Johns Hopkins University Press.

Joly, Henri. 1895. *Photozootrope à un plusieurs oculaires.* French patent 251,549. Filed November 8, 1895.

——. 1895a. *Nouvelle Appareil Chronophotographique.* French patent 249,875.

Josephson, Matthew. 1959. *Edison.* New York: McGraw-Hill.

Kahlbaum, Georg W. A. and Francis V. Darbishire, eds. 1899. *The Letters of Faraday and Schönbein.* Basel/London: Williams & Norgate.

Kamm, Leonard Ulrich. 1898. *Improvements in Apparatus for Photographing and Exhibiting Cinematographic Pictures.* UK patent 6515. Filed March 17, 1898. Issued December 3, 1898.

Kohlrausch, Ernst. 1881. *Physik des Turnens.* Hof: R. Lion Verlag.

——. 1890. *Photographischer Apparat für Serienaufnahmen.* German patent 57,133. Filed October 8, 1890. Issued August 8, 1891.

——. 1898. "Demonstrations-Vortrag über photographische Reihen-Aufnahmen vom Gange nervenkranker Personen und deren lebendiger Wiedergabe durch Projection." In *Verhandlungen des Congresses für Innere Medicin,* ed. E. Von Leyden and Emil Pfeiffer, 564–70. Wiesbaden: Verlag von J. F. Bergmann.

Korsten, Lucien, Georges Méliès and Lucien Reulos. 1896. *Appareil destiné prendre et à projeter les photographies animées.* French patent 259,444. Filed September 2, 1896.

Krayn, Robert. 1897. *Verfahren zur Aufnahme und Vorführung von Serienbildern.* German patent 107,373. Filed November 13, 1897. Issued November 30, 1899.

Lange-Fuchs, Hauke. 1987. *Birt Acres. Der erste schleswig-holsteinische Film Pionier*. Kiel: Walter G. Mühlau.

———. 1995. *Der Kaiser, der Kanal, und die Kinematogaphie*. (Veröffentlichungen des Schleswig-Holsteinischen Landesarchivs, vol. 42.) Schleswig: Landesarchiv Schleswig-Holstein.

———. 1995a. "On the Origin of Moving Slides." *New Magic Lantern Journal* 7.3 (November 1995): 10–14.

Latham, Woodville. 1896. [James Yates Johnson, patent agent] *Improvements in Means or Apparatus for Exhibiting Pictures of Moving Objects by Projecting Them on a Screen or Other Surface*. UK patent 4841. Filed March 3, 1896. Issued February 13, 1897.

———. 1896a. *Projecting Kinetoscope*. US patent 707,934. Filed June 1, 1896. Issued August 26, 1902.

Le Prince, Louis Aimé Augustin. 1888. *Method of and Apparatus for Producing Animated Pictures of Natural Scenery and Life*. US patent 376,247. Filed November 2, 1886. Issued January 10, 1888.

———. 1888a. *Improvements in the Method of and Apparatus for Producing Animated Photographic Pictures*. UK patent 423. Filed January 10, 1888. Issued November 16, 1888.

———. 1888b. *Méthode et appareil pour la projection des tableaux animées*. French patent 188,089. Issued January 11, 1888.

Liesegang, F. Paul. 1908. "Konstruktionstypen des Kinematographen." *Physikalische Zeitschrift* 9.22 (1908): 741–45.

Lincoln, William E. 1867. *Zoetrope*. US patent 64,117. Issued 23 April 1867.

Linnett, John Barnes. 1868. *Producing Optical Illusions*. UK patent 925. Filed March 18, 1868. Issued September 5, 1868.

Loiperdinger, Martin. 1996. "Lumière's *Ankunft des Zugs*. Gründungsmythos eines neuen Mediums." *KINtop* (Basel/Frankfurt am Main: Stroemfeld/Roter Stern) 5: 37–70.

Loiperdinger, Martin and Roland Cosandey, eds. 1992. *Des sous comme s'il en pleuvait. Quatre documents pour servir à l'histoire du Cinématographe*. Lausanne: Université de Lausanne, Faculté des Lettres, Histoire et esthétique du cinéma.

Lumière, Auguste and Louis. 1895. *Appareil servant à l'obtention et à la vision des épreuves chronophotographiques.* French patent 245,032. Filed February 13, 1895.

———. 1895a. *1re Addition en date du 30 mars 1895.* Addition to French patent 245,032.

———. 1896. *Appareil de vision directe des épreuves chronophotographiques dit "Kinora."* French patent 259,515. Filed September 10, 1896.

———. [Société anonyme des plaques et papiers photographiques A. Lumière et ses fils]. 1902. *Cinématographe à mouvement continu de la pellicule.* French patent 323,667. Filed on November 17, 1902. Issued March 11, 1903.

Mannoni, Laurent. 1994. *Le grand art de la lumière et de l'ombre. Archéologie du cinéma.* Paris: Éditions Nathan.

———. 1995. "Glissements progressifs vers le plaisir. Remarques sur l'œuvre chronophotographique de Marey et Demenÿ." *1895* 18 (Summer 1995): 11–50.

———. 1996. *Le mouvement continué. Catalogue illustré de la collection des appareils de la Cinémathèque française.* Paris: Mazzotta/Cinémathèque française.

———. 1997. *Georges Demenÿ. Pionnier du cinéma.* Boulogne-sur-Mer: Cinématheque française/Éditions Pagine/Université Lille 3.

———. 1997a. "Méliés contrefacteur?" *1895* 22 (July 1997): 17–22.

Marey, Étienne-Jules. 1863. *Physiologie médicale de la circulation du sang basée sur l'étude graphique des mouvements du coeur et du pouls artériel, avec application aux maladies de l'appareil circulatoire.* Paris: Delahaye.

———. 1874. *Animal Mechanism: A Treatise on Terrestrial and Aerial Locomotion.* London: H. S. King. English edition of *La Machine animale: Locomotion terrestre et aérienne.* Paris: Alcan, 1873.

———. 1895. *Movement.* (New York: Appleton. English edition of *Le Mouvement.* Paris: Masson, 1894).

Marvin, Harry N. 1895. *Mutoscope.* US patent 584,311. Filed November 14, 1895. Divided and this application filed May 26, 1896. Issued June 8, 1897.

Maskelyne, John Nevil. 1896. *An Improved Apparatus for Securing, or Exhibiting in Series, Records of Successive Phases of Movement.* UK patent 11,639. Filed on May 28, 1896. Issued May 1, 1897.

May, Charles W. 1867. *Instrument d'optique dit Zoetrope, propre à produire des illusions agréables et amusantes.* French patent 76,420. Issued May 14, 1867.

Millard, Andre. 1898. "Machine Shop Culture and Menlo Park." In *Working at Inventing: Thomas A. Edison and the Menlo Park Experience,* ed. William S. Pretzer, 48–65. Dearborn, MI: Henry Ford Museum/Greenfield Village.

Mortier, Paul. 1896. *Appareil dénomme Aléthoscope, destiné à enregistrer photographiquement les scènes animées et à les reproduire, soit par projection, soit par vision directe avec ou sans l'illusion du relief.* French patent 254,090. Filed on February 17, 1896. Plus addition of February 28, 1896.

Musser, Charles. 1990. *History of the American Cinema,* vol. 1: *The Emergence of Cinema: The American Screen to 1907.* (New York: Charles Scribner's Sons).

———. 1991. *Before the Nickelodeon: Edwin S. Porter and the Edison Manufacturing Company.* Berkeley/Los Angeles/Oxford: University of California Press.

Muybridge, Eadweard. 1878. *Improvement in the Method and Apparatus for Photographing Objects in Motion.* US patent 212,865. Filed on June 27, 1878.

———. 1878a. *Improvement in the Method and Apparatus for Photographing Objects in Motion.* US patent 212,864. Filed on July 11, 1878.

Parkes, Alexander. 1856. Provisional UK patent 1123. Not issued.

———. 1865. *Improvements in the Manufacture of Parkesine or Compounds of Pyroxyline, and also Solutions of Pyroxyline, known as Collodion.* UK patent 1313. Filed on May 11, 1865.

Pahl, Karl, 1933. "Aktennotiz über die Besprechung mit Herrn Pahl am 30. Mai 1933 vormittags 10 Uhr in Dahlem, Parkstrasse 56." Bundesarchiv (Berlin), Nachlaß Messter, NL Ex 275 (Ex-Akte 342).

Paul, Robert W. 1896. *Improvements in Apparatus for Projecting Kinetoscope Pictures on the Screen.* UK patent 4686. Filed March 2, 1896. Issued January 23, 1897.

——. 1936. "Kinematographic Experiences." In *A Technological History of Motion Pictures and Television*, ed. Raymond Fielding, 42–48. Berkeley: University of California Press. Reprinted from the *Journal of the Society of Motion Picture Engineers* 27 (November 1936).

Pickering, F. A. 1936. "Was Lumière First?" Letter of March 12, 1936 in *To-Day's Cinema*, March 13, 1936, pp. 1, 10.

Potter, E. T. 1888. UK patent 14,171. Filed October 2, 1888. Abandoned, not issued.

Rawlence, Christopher. 1990. *The Missing Reel: The Untold Story of the Lost Inventor of Moving Pictures*. London: Collins.

Reichenbach, Henry M. 1889. *Manufacture of Flexible Photographic Films*. US patent 417,202. Filed on April 9, 1889.

Reynaud, Émile. 1877. *Appareil pour obtenir l'illusion du mouvement à l'aide de glaces mobiles*. French patent 120,484. Issued August 30, 1877.

——. 1888. *Appareil dit Théâtre optique*. French patent 194,482. Issued December 1, 1888.

Rittaud-Hutinet, Jacques. 1985. *Le cinéma des origines. Les frères Lumière et leurs opérateurs*. Seyssel: Champ Vallon.

——. 1990. *Auguste et Louis Lumière. Les 1000 premiers films*. Paris: Philippe Sers éditeur/Vilo diffusion.

——, ed. 1995. *Letters. Auguste and Louis Lumière*. London/Boston: Faber & Faber. (Note: readers using this book in English should be aware of substantial mistranslations of technical terms in correspondence between the Lumières and their mechanic Carpentier during the evolution of the Cinématographe, one of the most important topics of these letters, which make the descriptions almost unintelligible.

——. 1995a. *Les Frères Lumière. L'invention du cinéma*. Paris: Flammarion.

Rossell, Deac. 1995. "The Old Thing with the Long Name and the New Thing with the Name That Isn't Much Shorter: A Cinema Chronology, 1889–1896." *Film History* (special issue) 7.2 (Summer 1995): 115–236.

———. 1995a. "'Lebende Bilder.' Die Chronophotographen Ottomar Anschütz und Ernst Kohlrausch." *Wir Wunderkinder. 100 Jahre Filmproduktion in Niedersachsen,* ed. Pamela Müller and Susanne Höbermann. Hannover: Gesellschaft für Filmstudien e. V.

———. 1996. "Eadweard Muybridge et la culture de l'image en mouvement." In *Actes de l'Colloque Marey/Muybridge, pionniers du cinéma,* ed. Marion Leuba. Beaune: Musée Marey/Réunion des Musées Nationaux.

———. 1997. "Jenseits von Messter—die ersten Berliner Kinematographen-Anbieter." *KINtop* (Basel/Frankfurt am Main: Storemfeld/Roter Stern) 6 (Autumn 1997): 167–84.

———. 1997a. *Ottomar Anschütz and his Electrical Wonder.* London: The Projection Box.

Sadoul, Georges. 1946. *Histoire générale du cinéma. I: L'invention du cinéma 1832– 1897.* Paris: Éditions Denoël.

———. 1964. *Louis Lumière.* Cinéma d'aujourd'hui, No. 29. Paris: Éditions Seghers.

Schmidt, F. A. 1887. "Die Augenblicksphotographie und ihre Bedeutung für die Bewegungslehre." *Deutsche Turn-Zeitung* (Leipzig) 51 (December 22, 1887): 759–64.

Schönbein, Christian Frederick. 1846a. [John Taylor] *Improvements in the Manufacture of Explosive Compounds.* UK patent 11,407. Filed October 8, 1846. Issued April 8, 1847.

———. 1846b. *Improvement in Preparation of Cotton-Wool and Other Substances as Substitutes for Gun-Powder.* US patent 4,874. Issued on December 5, 1846.

Schwartz, Arthur. 1892. Brochure describing the Tachyscope of Ottomar Anschütz, n.d. (1892), 4pp., New York. (Collection Cinémathèque Française)

Siemens & Halske. 1893. Letter of November 7, 1893 from the Charlottenburg Werke to G. Fleischhauer & Co, Magdeburg. Siemens-Archiv, Akte 25/LO108.

Skladanowsky, Max. 1895. *Vorrichtung zum intermittirenden Vorwärtsbewegen des Bildbandes für photographische Serien Apparate und Bioskope.* German patent 88,599. Filed November 1, 1895. Issued October 21, 1896.

Spill, Daniel. 1869. *Improved Method of Making Solid Collodion.* US patent 91,377. Filed March 18, 1869. Issued December 8, 1869.

——. 1869a. *Preparing and Using Solvents of Xyloidine.* UK patent 3102. Filed October 26, 1869. Issued April 19, 1870.

Stevens, John H. 1882. *Manufacture of Compounds of Pyroxyline or Nitro-cellulose.* US patent 269,340. Filed on June 12, 1882.

Talbot, Frederick A. 1912. *Moving Pictures: How They Are Made and Worked.* London: William Heinemann.

Tate, Alfred O. 1938. *Edison's Open Door.* New York: Dutton & Company.

Varley, Frederick Henry. 1890. *Improvements in Cameras for Photographing Objects in Motion.* UK patent 4704. Filed March 26, 1890. Issued February 28, 1891.

Wachhorst, Wyn. 1981. *Thomas Alva Edison: An American Myth.* Cambridge, MA: MIT Press.

Wray, Cecil. 1895. *Improvements in Apparatus for Exhibiting Kinetoscopic or Zoetropic Pictures.* UK Patent 182. Filed on January 3, 1895. Issued on December 7, 1895.

——. 1896. *Improvements in Apparatus for Exhibiting Kinetoscopic or Zoetropic Pictures.* UK patent 19,181. Filed on August 31, 1896. Issued June 12, 1897.

Zglinicki, Friedrich von. 1979. *Der Weg des Films,* 2 vols. Hildesheim/ New York, 1979 (1956): Olms Presse.

INDEX

1492 (Edison), 146
Abe Edgington, 32
Acres, Birt, 70, 74, 92–94, 135, 139,
    142, 146, 147, 151
    Birtac, 151
Adams, Walter Poynter, 64
AEG Company (Allgemeine
    Elektrizitäts Gesellschaft), 158
Akrobatisches Potpourri
    (Skladanowsky), 115
Albany, New York, 61
Allister, Ray, 106
Alma-Tadema, Lawrence, 39
American Mutoscope and Biograph
    Co., 110
American Mutoscope and Biograph
    Company, 98, 100, 148,
    158–61
    Biograph projector, 160
Amsterdam, The Netherlands, 89
Ançion, Mlle., 115
Anderton, John, 118
Angerer, Ludwig, 42
Animatoscope (Eames), 112
Annan, John, 48
Anschütz, Ottomar, 27, 41–44,
    46–49, 55, 59, 83, 86, 90, 106,
    116, 118, 120, 121, 143
    Electrical Schnellseher, 44–48,
    83, 90, 116, 118, 120, 131,146
    Electrical Tachyscope, 44, 83

Projecting Electrotachyscope,
    47, 120
Ansco Company, 68, 74
Anthony & Scoville Company, 32
Apotheose (Skladanowsky), 115
Archer, Frederick Scott, 59, 65
Archerotype, 59
Armat, Hunter, 121
Armat, Thomas, 52, 71, 75, 92, 110,
    119–21, 123, 143, 144, 161
    Phantoscope, 121, 123, 126, 127,
    144
    Vitascope, 52, 144, 146, 161
Arrest of a Pickpocket, The (Paul),
    93
Atkinson, T. W., 15
Atlanta, Georgia, 120, 121, 123,
    126, 144

Bain d'une mondaine, Le (Joly), 131
Balagny, Georges, 41
Balagny, Victor, 72
Bamforth & Co., 24
Barbershop Scene (Edison), 128,
    146
Barnes, John, 146, 155
Barnet, England, 74, 92
Barnett, Charles, 125, 126
Barnett, Harry Walter, 136
Barr, Captain H. J., 65
Basel, Switzerland, 58

179

Bath, England, 106, 107
Baucus, Joseph D., 89
Beale, J., 17
Beaune, France, 35
Bedts, George William de, 54, 55, 131
Bell, Alexander Graham, 80
Berlin, Germany, 9, 42, 44, 46–48, 50, 76, 94, 112–13, 115, 117, 140, 147, 158
Bettini, G., 11
Beyrich, Ferdinand, 42
Bijker, Wiebe E., 4–6, 11
Biograph camera (Casler), 97, 159
Biograph projector (Casler), 160–62
Biographé (Demenÿ), 55
Biokam (Darling & Wrench), 151
Biomatograph (Foersterling), 147
Bioskop (Skladanowsky), 8, 9, 113, 115–18
Bioskop II (Skladanowsky), 9, 113
Birmingham, England, 118
Birtac (Acres), 151
Black Maria (studio, Edison), 86, 88, 91, 123
Black, Alexander, 24
Blackpool, England, 117, 118
Blair Camera Company, 58, 65, 69–71, 86
Blair, John Henry, 138
Blair, Thomas Henry, 69–72, 74
    Blair Camera Company, 58
    European Blair Camera Company, 58
    Hawk-Eye camera, 138
Bohr, Nils, 21
Bolas, Thomas, 109
Bonelli, Gaetano, 28
Bonnat, Leon, 38
Booth, Edwin, 82
Booth, Walter, 142
Boston Camera Club (US), 112
Boston, Massachusetts, 46, 48, 69, 112, 120, 121
Boulogne-sur-Mer, France, 72

Boxende Kanguruh, Das (Skladanowsky), 115
Boxing Kangaroo, The (Acres), 93
Braconnot, Henri, 58
Bradford, England, 6, 119, 157
Bragaglia, Anton Giulio, 36
Braun, Marta, 39, 41
Bremen, Germany, 48
Bristol, England, 107
Brooklyn Institute, 86, 90
Brooklyn, New York, 161
Brown, Arthur, 32
Brown, Charles A., 82
Brown, O. B., 17
Brussels, Belgium, 131, 135
Budapest, Hungary, 112
Bull, Lucien, 162
Bundesarchiv, Berlin, 113
Bünzli, Rene, 10–11, 151
Burlington, Vermont, 74

Canastoda, New York, 96
Canton, Ohio, 161
Carbutt, John, 63, 64, 82
    Keystone Dry Plate Company, 63
Carpentier, Jules, 74, 131, 135, 139
Casler, Herman, 75, 94, 96, 119, 150, 159
    Biograph Camera, 97
    Biograph projector, 160, 161
    K.C.M.D. group, 95–97
    Mutoscope, 96–98
    Photoret camera, 94, 98
Celluloid Manufacturing Company, 61–62, 64, 69–70, 75, 89
Centre national de la cinématographie, 129
Cerf, Camille, 135
Chapuis, Marius, 136
Charles, Louis, 140
Chicago, Illinois, 40, 46, 88, 90, 104, 120, 126
Childe, Henry Langdon, 13–14
Chinnock, Charless E., 91

Choreutoscope, 17, 86, 107, 148, 155
Chronophotographe (Demenÿ), 55
Chronophotographe (Gaumont/Demenÿ), 161
CinemaScope 55, 162
Cinémathèque Française, 41
Cinématographe (Lumière), 9, 48, 54, 72, 93, 116–17, 127, 129–32, 135–36, 138–40, 148–51
Clarke, William Gibbs, 51
Claudet, A. Francois J., 28
Clément-Maurice, 128, 132
Cody, Buffalo Bill, 88
Coe, Brian, 106
Collings, Esme, 107
Cologne, Germany, 92, 93
Columbia Phonograph Company, 123
Columbian Exposition, Chicago, 40, 46, 90, 120
Comic Shoeblack, The (Paul) 93
Concerthaus, Hamburg, 116
Continental Commerce Company (Maguire & Baucus), 89
Continsouza, Pierre-Victor, 10–11, 147, 151
Cook, Henry, 28
Corbett, James, 91, 124
Cotton States Exhibition, Atlanta, 120, 126, 144
Courtney, Peter, 91
Cricks, G. H., 142
Crystal Palace (London), 92
Cushing, Jack, 91, 123
Cushing, Peter, 124
Cutting, James A., 59

Daguerre, J. L. M., 104
Daguerreotype, 29, 59
Dallmeyer, Thomas Rudolf, 32
Darling, Alfred, 151
Biokam, 151
Débarquement du congres de photographie à Lyon, Le, 132
Demaria, Jules, 54

Demenÿ, Georges, 28, 36, 50–52, 54–55, 86, 89–91, 106, 120–21, 127, 129, 131, 135, 161
Biographe, 55
Chronophotographe, 55, 161
Phonoscope, 51–52, 54–55, 89–91, 94, 135
Société Général du Phonoscope, 51, 54
Desvignes, Peter Henry, 28
Deutsch-Österreichischen-Edison-Kinetoskop-Gesellschaft, 89
Deutsches Automaten Gesellschaft, 135
Deutsches Museum, Munich, 49
Devant, David, 9, 76, 140
Dickson, William Kennedy Laurie, 57, 63, 69, 79, 82–83, 85–86, 88, 94–99, 101, 103, 118, 124, 126, 158–60
Biograph Camera, 97
K.C.M.D. group, 95–97
Kinetograph camera, 159–60
Photoret camera, 94, 98
Dijon, France, 105
Douai, France, 50
Doublier, Francis, 136
Duboscq, Jules, 28, 39
Duchamp, Marcel, 36
Ducos du Hauron, Louis Arthur, 29
Dupont, Eugène, 135–36, 138
Duval, Mathias, 35

E. & H.T. Anthony, 65
Eakins, Thomas, 28, 34, 48
Eames, Owen A., 112
Animatoscope, 112
Eastman Company, 104, 108, 125
Eastman Dry Plate Company, 58, 65, 67, 71, 85
Eastman Kodak Company, 40, 68–69, 72, 77
Eastman, George, 64–71, 138
Eastman Dry Plate, 65
Eastman Dry Plate Company, 58
Kodak camera, 138

Eclipse Kinematoscope Office, 155

Eden Musee, 14, 16, 46

Edison Projecting Home Kinetoscope, 77

Edison, Mrs. Minna, 83

Edison, Thomas Alva, 44, 57, 62–63, 69, 75, 79–86, 88–92, 96–101, 103, 106–7, 110, 118–21, 124–28, 133–34, 139, 143–44, 146–48, 159

   Black Maria, 86, 88, 91

   Kinesigraph camera, 83–84, 97, 106

   Kinetograph camera, 159–60

   Kinetoscope, 6, 44, 80–86, 88–91, 94, 96–101, 103, 116, 118–21, 123–24, 126–29, 135, 139, 144, 146, 148, 157, 160

   Projecting Home Kinetoscope, 77

   Vitascope, 52, 144, 146, 161

Edison's Ideal (Foersterling), 147

Egyptian Hall, London, 158

Eidoloscope (Latham), 124, 126–27, 143

Einstein, Albert, 21

Electrical Schnellseher (Anschütz), 46–47, 146

Electrical Tachyscope (Anschütz), 44

Electrical Wonder Company, London, 46–47

Elliott and Son, Barnet, 92

Empire Theatre, London, 116–17

England, William, 64

Erfinder des Bioscops, Der (Skladanowsky), 115

European Blair Camera Company, 54, 58, 70–72, 129, 132

Evans, Mortimer, 108

Faraday, Michael, 58

Feddersen, Bernhard Wilhelm, 28

Feyzin, France, 74

Filmmuseum, Potsdam, 113

Foersterling, Herman O., 94, 147

   Biomatograph, 147

   Edison's Ideal, 147

Folies Bergère, Paris, 116–17

Foot's Cray, Kent, England, 70

Forgerons, Les (Lumière), 132

Frankfurt am Main, Germany, 15, 44, 46

Franz-Joseph I, Kaiser, 138

Freeman, James P., 119

Friedrich III, King of Prussia, 44

Friese Greene, William, 85, 106–9

Gabriel Grubb (lantern show), 14

Gammon, Frank R., 88, 144

Gaumont Company, 149, 161

Gaumont, Léon, 55, 132

Gee, A. J., 142

Georgiades, George, 92

Gilmore, William, 97, 144

Girel, François-Constant, 136

glass plate cinematography, 10, 151–52

Goodwin Film & Camera Company, 68, 74

Goodwin, Rev. Hannibal Williston, 64, 68–69, 74

Gray, Gustav le, 59

Gray, Robert Dempsey, 109–10

Greenwich, England, 17

Griffiths, Albert, 125–26

Grünewald, Arthur, 135

Grünewald, Ivan, 135

Hagedorn Company, 112

Hagotype Company, 68

Hale's Tours, 93

Hamann, Johann, 94

Hamburg, Germany, 94, 116

Hammerstein's Olympia Theater, New York , 161

Hanfstaengl, Franz, 42

Hanover, Germany, 43, 49

Hard Wash, A (Biograph), 161

Hartford, Connecticut, 10

Hawk-Eye camera (Blair), 138

Heise, William, 83, 85, 88
Hendricks, Gordon, 83
Hepworth, Cecil, 17
Hertz, Carl, 140, 142
Hick Brothers, 104
Hill, W. R., 14
Hoffmann, Paul, 15
Holland, Holland, 88
Hopkins, George M., 86
Horner, William George, 19
Hough, James Edward, 91
Hughes, Thomas P., 80–81
Hughes, William Charles, 17, 52,
    154–55
    Motor-Pictoroscope, 155
    Photo-Rotoscope, 153, 155
    Street Cinematograph, 153, 155
Hunt, Holman, 39
Hyatt, Isaiah Smith, 61–63
Hyatt, John Wesley, 61–63

Imax system, 162
Inahata, Shotaro, 135
Isaacs, John D., 32
Italienischer Bauerntanz
    (Skladanowsky), 115
Ivens, C. A. P., 89

J. Otway and Sons, 155
Janssen, Pierre Jules César, 29, 32,
    36
    Révolver Astronomique, 29
Jardinier, Le (Lumière), 132
Jefferson, Joseph, 161
Jenkins, C. Francis, 92, 110,
    119–21, 123, 143, 144
    Phantoscope, 120–21, 123,
    126–27, 144
Johannesburg, South Africa, 140
Joinville (Paris), France, 55, 119
Joly, Henri, 92, 119, 131, 132
    Photozootrope, 119
Jongleur, Der (Skladanowsky), 115
Joy, Henry W., 151
    Spirograph, 151
Jumeau, Émile, 62

K.C.M.D. group, 95–97, 159
Kamarinskija (Skladanowsky), 115
Kamm, Leonard Ulrich, 11, 151
    Kammatograph, 151
    Kammatograph (Kamm), 151
Keith, Benjamin Franklin, 161
Keith's Union Square Theatre, New
    York, 160
Keystone Dry Plate Company, 63
Kiel, Germany, 94
Kindler, Emil, 48
Kinématographe (Méliès & Reulos),
    48
Kineoptoscope (Wray), 6, 8, 155,
    157, 159
Kinetograph camera (Edison),
    83–84, 97, 106, 159–60
Kinetoscope (Chinnock), 91
Kinetoscope (Edison), 6, 44, 57, 62,
    69–71, 75, 80–86, 88–91, 94,
    96–101, 103, 116, 118–21,
    123–24, 126–29, 135, 139, 144,
    146, 148, 157, 160
Kinetoscope (Paul), 139, 142
Kinetoscope Company (Raff &
    Gammon), 89
Kinetoscope Exhibition Company
    (Latham), 91, 124
King of Prussia, 42
Kingston Museum, Kingston-upon-
    Thames, England, 39
Kingston, England, 31, 39
Kinora (Lumière), 138, 148–50
Kodak camera, 138
Kohlrausch, Ernst, 28, 49, 50,
    55–56
Komisches Reck (Skladanowsky),
    115
Koopman, Elias Bernard, 94
    K.C.M.D. group, 95–97
    Magic Introduction Company,
    95–96, 98
Koster & Bial's Music Hall, New
    York, 46, 143, 146
Krayn, Robert, 152
Kupka, František, 36

Lambda Company (Latham), 97, 99, 124, 126
Lange-Fuchs, Hauke, 92
Langenheim, Frederick, 24
Langenheim, William, 24
Larkyns, Harry, 31
Latham, Gray, 97–98, 119, 123–27
  Eidoloscope, 124, 126–27
  Lambda Company, 97, 99, 124, 126
Latham, LeRoy, 127
Latham, Otway, 91, 97–98, 119, 123–27
  Eidoloscope, 124, 126–27
  Lambda Company, 97, 99, 124, 126
Latham, Woodville, 97–98, 119, 123–27
  Eidoloscope, 124, 126–27
  Lambda Company, 97, 99, 124, 126
Lauste, Eugene, 83, 124, 126
Lavanchy-Clarke, François-Henri, 135
Lavanchy-Clarke, William Gibbs, 54
Le Havre, France, 140
Leeds, England, 104
Leitz-Kinowerke, 158
Leonard, Michael, 91, 123
Le Prince, Louis Aimé Augustin, 85, 104–6
Levallois-Perret, France, 53
Liesegang, F. Paul, 158
Lilienthal, Otto, 42
Lille, France, 50
Lioret, Henri, 62
Lioretgraph, 62
Lipe, C. E., 94, 96
Lissa, East Prussia, 42
Loiperdinger, Martin, 92
Lomax, Alfred, 118
Londe, Albert, 28, 48–49
London and Provincial Photographic Association, 108
London Photographic Society, 63

London, England, 4, 9, 10, 14, 16–17, 46–47, 60, 70, 76, 89, 92–94, 104, 107–8, 116–18, 139–40, 142–43, 155, 157–58
Louvain, Belgium, 131
Lübeck, Germany, 146–47
Lumière Company (Société A. Lumiere et Fils), 54, 128, 129, 132
Lumière, Antoine, 128, 131–32, 135, 138, 144
Lumière, Auguste, 48, 70, 72, 74–75, 89, 116–17, 119, 127–28, 131, 133–36, 138–39, 142, 147, 148, 150–52, 157, 162
  Cinématographe, 48, 54, 93, 129–32, 135, 136, 138–40, 148–51
  Kinora, 138, 148–50
Lumière, Louis, 48, 54, 70, 72, 74–75, 89, 116–17, 119, 127–29, 131, 133–36, 138–39, 142, 147–48, 150–52, 157, 162–63
  Cinématographe, 48, 54, 93, 127, 129–32, 135–36, 138–40, 148–51
  Kinora, 138, 148–50
Lyon, France, 54, 72, 74, 127–28, 131, 135–36

Mach, Ernst, 28, 48
Magic Box, The (Boulting), 106
Magic Introduction Company, New York, 94, 96, 98
Magic lantern
  influence of, on cinema, 6
magic lantern show
  influence of, on film apparatus, 152, 154–55, 157–58
Maguire and Baucus, 89, 91
Maguire, Frank Z., 89
Mannoni, Laurent, 54
Marcy, Lorenzo J., 24
  Sciopticon lantern, 24, 68

Marey, Étienne-Jules, 27–28, 31–32, 34–36, 38, 40–42, 48–54, 72, 83, 94, 100, 119, 121, 127, 129, 143, 162
Martin, J. H., 142
Marvin, Harry, 94, 96
K.C.M.D. group, 95–97
Maskelyne, John Nevil, 140, 157–58
Mutagraph, 158
Maynard, J. Parker, 59
McCormick, Cyrus Hall, 80, 119
McKinley, William, 161
Mechau, Emil, 12, 158
Méliès, Georges, 6, 48, 132, 135, 140, 142
Kinématographe, 48
Mer, La (Lumière), 132
Mesguich, Felix, 136
Messter, Oskar, 6, 70, 113, 117, 140, 142
Milburn, Gustav, 67
Milk White Flag, The (Edison), 146
Millais, John Everett, 39
Miss Jerry (lantern play), 24
Mobisson, Ferdinand, 105
Moisson, Charles, 128–29, 132
Molteni lamp, 75
Morgan and Kidd, 65
Morse, Samuel, 80
Mortier, Paul, 157
Motion Picture Patents Company, 80, 101, 139
Motor-Pictoroscope (Hughes), 155
Müller, Paul, 94
Munich, Germany, 42–43, 49
Musée Grevin, 89
Musger, Anton, 158
Musschenbroek, Pieter van, 17, 162
Musser, Charles, 85, 88, 100, 104
Mutagraph (Maskelyne), 158
Mutoscope (Casler), 96–98, 159
Muybridge, Eadweard, 27, 29, 31–32, 34–35, 38–40, 42–43, 48–49, 51, 59, 82, 86, 88, 90, 100, 109, 143
Zoöpraxiscope, 34–35, 39, 51

Naples, Italy, 50
National Film and Television Archive, London, 93
New York, New York, 14, 16, 24, 31, 46–47, 61, 68, 88, 90–91, 104, 109, 123, 126, 143, 146, 157, 161
Newark, New Jersey, 61, 64, 68, 74–75, 86
Niagra Falls, New York, 127
Norfolk, Virginia, 127
Northern Photographic Works, 74

Occident, 31, 32
Omnimax system, 162
optical intermittent systems, 11
optical intermittents, 157, 158
Orange, New Jersey, 82
Orton, William, 84
Ott, Fred, 88
Oxford and Cambridge Boat Race (Acres/Paul), 92

Pahl, Karl, 9, 76
Painlève, Jean, 162
Palo Alto, California, 32
Panavision 70, 162
Pankow (Berlin), Germany, 115
Paris, France, 10, 21, 35, 40, 48, 50–51, 53–55, 75–76, 83, 89, 91–92, 105, 116–17, 132, 135–36, 139–40, 147
Parkes, Alexander, 59–61, 63
Parkesine, 59–60
Pathé Freres, 77
Pathé, Charles, 92, 131
Paul, Robert William, 2, 6, 8, 70, 75, 91–93, 119, 131, 133–34, 139–40, 142–43, 146–48, 150
reproduction kinetoscope, 6, 139
Theatrograph, 8, 139–40, 142, 159
Pêche aux poissons rouges, La (Lumière), 132
Pelouze, Theophile-Jules, 58
Péynaud, Alphonse, 42
Phantoscope (Jenkins), 120

Phantoscope (Jenkins/Armat),
    120–21, 123, 126–27, 144
Phelan & Collender, 61
Phenakistiscope, 19, 34, 39, 86, 103
Philadelphia, Pennsylvania, 24, 38,
    48, 63, 126, 161
Phonoscope (Demenÿ), 51–52,
    54–55, 86, 89–91, 94, 135
Photo-Rotoscope (Hughes), 155
Photoret Camera (Casler/Dickson),
    94, 98
Photozootrope (Joly), 119
Pickering, F. A., 117, 118
Pittsburgh, Pennsylvania, 161
Place des Cordeliers à Lyon, La
    (Lumière), 132
Planchon, Victor, 58, 72, 74, 129
Plateau, Joseph, 19, 28, 86
Plymouth, England, 107
Poggendorf, J. C., 58
Porter, D. C., 126
Potter, E. T., 64
Prague, Czech Republic, 48, 146
Praxinoscope, 21, 148, 158
Praxinoscope Theatre, 21
Preller, Friedrich, 15
Prestwich Manufacturing
    Company, 52, 155
Projecting Electrotachyscope
    (Anschütz), 47
Projecting Home Kinetoscope
    (Edison), 77
Promio, Jean Alexandre Louis, 136
pyroxyline, 58, 59, 66

Raff & Gammon, 89, 91, 144, 146,
    161
Raff, Norman C., 88
Rastatt, Germany, 158
Rector, Enoch J., 91, 124
Reichenbach, Harry M., 67–68
Repas, Le (Lumière), 132
Révolver Astronomique (Janssen),
    29
Reynaud, Émile, 11, 21, 158
    Praxinoscope, 21, 158

Praxinoscope Theatre, 21
Théâtre Optique, 21, 158
Richmond, Indiana, 123
Riley Brothers, Bradford, 6, 155,
    157
    Kineoptoscope, 6, 157
Ringkampf zwischen Greiner und
    Sandow (Skladanowsky), 115
Rip Van Winkle (Biograph) 161
Rittaud-Hutinet, Jacques, 132
Rives Company, 66
Robinson, Archibald, 28
Rochester, New York, 64, 126
Ross, Thomas, 51
Rough Seas at Dover (Acres/Paul)
    146
Rousby, Edwin, 142
Rudge, John Arthur Roebuck,
    107–9
Rühmkorff, Heinrich Daniel, 131
Russell, Lillian, 82

Sallie Gardner, 32
San Francisco, California, 31–32,
    34, 88
Sandow, Eugene, 88, 161
Saut à la couverture, Le (Lumière),
    132
Schneider, 42, 44
Schnellseher (Anschütz), 44–48, 83,
    90, 116, 118, 120, 131
Schönbein, Christian Friedrich,
    58–59
Schwartz, Arthur, 46–47
Science Museum, London, 104
Sciopticon Lantern, 24, 68
Sébert, Général, 49
Serpentine Dance (Edison) 146
Serpentintanz (Skladanowsky),
    115
Sestier, Marius, 136
Sheepshead Bay, New York, 127
Short, Henry, 92, 142
Showscan (Trumbull), 160
Siemens & Halske, 46–48
Skladanowsky, Carl, 112

Skladanowsky, Emil, 8, 112–13,
    116–17
  Bioskop, 117
Skladanowsky, Max, 8–9, 48, 75,
    112–13, 115–18
  Bioskop, 9, 113, 115–18
  Bioskop II, 9, 113
Slater, Dundas, 117
Smith, Dr. J. H. & Co., 74
Smith, Jack, 142
Société A. Lumière et Fils, 135–36,
    138–39
Société Charité Maternelle, 10, 75
Société de la photographie animée,
    135
Société Général du Phonoscope, 51,
    54
Soldier's Courtship, The (Paul) 142
Sortie d'usine (Lumière), 132
Sousa, John Phillip, 88
Spill, Daniel, 60, 63
Spirograph (Joy), 151
Stable on Fire (Biograph), 161
Stampfer, Simon, 19
Stanford, Leland, 31–32, 34, 48
Stevens, John H., 64
Steward, James Henry, 17
Stollwerck Company, 48, 51, 74,
    89, 94, 135, 147
    Deutsche Automaten
    Gesellschaft, 135
Stollwerck, Ludwig, 93, 135
Street Cinematograph (Hughes),
    153, 155
Sutton, Thomas, 28
Sydney, Australia, 89, 136
Syracuse, New York, 94, 126

Tachyscope (Anschütz), 44, 83
Tate, Alfred O., 88, 99
Technirama, 162
Tegetmeier, W. B., 34
Théâtre Optique (Reynaud), 11, 21,
    158
Theatrograph (Paul), 8, 139–40,
    142, 159

Thompson, William Gilman,
    48
Todd-AO, 162
Tragides, George, 92
Trewey, Felicien, 135, 139
Trouville, France, 142
Trumbull, Douglas, 160
Turner, Samuel N., 69

Udine, Italy, 146
Umbrella Dance (Edison) 146
Urban, Charles, 150–51
Utrecht, The Netherlands, 17

Vandergrift, 126
Varley, Frederick, 108
Verständig, Anton, 47
Veyre, Gabriel, 136
Vienna, Austria, 42, 112, 135–36
Vincennes, France, 131
Vitascope (Edison/Armat), 52, 71,
    144, 146, 161
Voltige, La (Lumière), 132

Wagner, Richard, 15
Walker, William H., 65
Warnerke, Leon, 65
Warwick Trading Company,
    150–51, 155
Washington, D. C., 24, 104, 119–20,
    123
Wealdstone, England, 67
Weigel, Erhard, 17
Wells, Herbert George, 93
Welton, Harry, 88
Werner, Michel and Eugene, 89, 91,
    128
West Orange, New Jersey, 63, 80,
    82–83, 88, 90, 96, 98–99, 101,
    121, 146
Western Union Company, 84
Wheatstone, Charles, 28
Wheel of Life (Ross), 51, 107
Whistler, James Macneil, 38
Whitford, Annabelle, 88
Wiesbaden, Germany, 55

Wintergarten Theatre, Berlin,
115–18
Wood, E. G., 64, 72
Woolwich Arsenal, 158
Woolwich, England, 158
Wray, Cecil, 6, 8, 119, 155, 157
Kineoptoscope, 6, 157, 159
Wrench, Alfred, 151
Biokam, 151

xyloidine, 58

York and Son, England, 24, 25
Young Griffo, 125, 126

Zoetrope, 19, 21, 86
Zoöpraxiscope (Muybridge), 34, 35,
39, 51
Zurich, Switzerland, 74